TECUMSEH
AND THE
SHAWNEE
CONFEDERATION

▲

LIBRARY OF AMERICAN
INDIAN HISTORY

TECUMSEH AND THE SHAWNEE CONFEDERATION

▲

Rebecca Stefoff

☑®

Facts On File, Inc.

Tecumseh and the Shawnee Confederation

Facts On File, Inc.
11 Penn Plaza
New York NY 10001

Library of Congress Cataloging-in-Publication Data

Stefoff, Rebecca, 1951–
    Tecumseh and the Shawnee confederation / Rebecca Stefoff.
        p.   cm. — (Library of American Indian history)
    Includes bibliographical references and index.
    ISBN 0-8160-3648-9
    1. Tecumseh, Shawnee Chief, 1768–1813—Juvenile literature.
    2. Shawnee   Indians—Kings and rulers—Biography—Juvenile
    literature. 3. Shawnee Indians—Government relations—Juvenile
    literature. 4. Shawnee Indians—Wars, 1775–1783—Juvenile
    literature.   I. Title.   II. Series.
    E99.S35T345   1998
    977'.004973'0092—dc21
    [B]   97-22773

Facts On File books are available at special discounts when purchased in bulk quantities for businesses, associations, institutions or sales promotions. Please call our Special Sales Department in New York at (212) 967-8800 or (800) 322-8755.

You can find Facts On File on the World Wide Web at
http://www.factsonfile.com

Text design by Robert Yaffe
Series and cover design by Amy Beth Gonzalez
Cover design by Sholto Ainslie
Maps on pages 28, 63, and 102 by Dale Williams

This book is printed on acid-free paper.

Printed in the United States of America

MP FOF 10 9 8 7 6 5 4 3 2 1

CONTENTS

▲

STANDOFF AT GROUSELAND

1

The Wabash River flowed sluggishly through southern Indiana in the summer of 1810. By midafternoon on Sunday, August 12, the birds and animals who lived along the river's banks were holed up in shady spots, sleeping through the hottest part of the day. The only sound or motion came from the dusty leaves hanging limply over the water. From time to time they rustled in a breath of air that was too faint to be called a breeze.

Around a bend in the river came a fleet of Indian canoes. Accounts of that day's events differ on how many canoes and Indians there were; the canoes probably numbered about eighty and were carrying about two or three hundred Indians. Their appearance banished all drowsiness from Fort Knox, the U.S. Army post on that stretch of the river. Although the officers and men of Fort Knox had been expecting the Indians, they were surprised—and a bit alarmed—to see such a large group of painted, rifle-carrying warriors.

Captain George Floyd was the commanding officer of Fort Knox. It was his job to inspect all river traffic, so he ordered the canoes to stop. Two days later, in a letter to a friend in Louisville, Floyd recounted that the Indians were "well prepared for war in case of an attack." He also described their leader as "one of the finest looking men I ever saw—about six feet high, straight, with large fine features and altogether a daring bold-looking fellow."

That leader was forty-two-year-old Tecumseh, a war chief of the Shawnee people. He was on his way to a meeting with William Henry Harrison, the governor of the Indiana Territory. Captain

Drawn by a trader who knew Tecumseh, this is considered the most accurate likeness of the Shawnee leader. A British officer later added the medal of King George III, which Tecumseh sometimes wore, and a British officer's coat, which he probably never wore. *(Indiana Historical Society, negative C6629)*

Floyd was under orders to attend that meeting, too. Perhaps, as he looked at Tecumseh and his warriors approaching the fort in the glaring sunlight, with the brown waters of the Wabash rippling and gurgling under the bows of their canoes, Floyd realized that he was going to witness a historic encounter. Tecumseh was a much-feared, almost legendary war leader who was determined to keep white settlers out of the Indian lands north of the Ohio River. Harrison, five years younger than Tecumseh, was a brave former soldier and a stern governor who was determined to see those same lands settled and made into states. The two men had opposed one another for years. Now their first face-to-face meeting was at hand.

After a brief inspection, Floyd allowed Tecumseh and his men to pass the fort. The Shawnee camped two miles downstream. The meeting would begin on August 15 at Grouseland, Harrison's home in the settlement of Vincennes, a mile below the Shawnee camp.

Grouseland was a slice of civilized comfort in a frontier country that was still largely untamed. It was a brick mansion of thirteen rooms, set within beautifully landscaped gardens. Inside, the house boasted polished wooden floors, an elegant sweeping staircase to the second floor, a mahogany grand piano, and sparkling glass chandeliers, all tended by uniformed slaves. Harrison had named the place for the game birds called ruffed grouse that abounded on its grounds.

On the day appointed for the meeting, Harrison waited for Tecumseh on the porch of Grouseland. With him were a handful of the traders and frontiersmen who served Harrison as interpreters, messengers, and spies in his dealings with the Indians; Winamac, a Potawatomi chieftain who had signed a treaty with Harrison and had become an ally of the whites; some leading local citizens and members of the territorial government; a few military officers, including Captain Floyd; and a squad of armed soldiers. They were there to present a strong, united front to the visiting Shawnee. Harrison intended to impress Tecumseh with the power and authority of the territorial government so that the Shawnee leader would bend to Harrison's will. Already, however, the meeting was not going as the governor had planned.

A month or so earlier, Harrison had issued an invitation not to Tecumseh but to Tecumseh's brother to meet at Grouseland.

Known as the Shawnee Prophet, the brother was a religious leader, not a fighter. He was a much less intimidating and worrisome figure than the fierce Tecumseh. Yet the Prophet had refused to come, and Tecumseh announced that *he* would come instead. Harrison, who wanted to take over the territory peacefully rather than through continual fighting, could not refuse. He could, however, try to prevent a large Indian force from entering Vincennes, so he sent messages stating that he would welcome Tecumseh and a *few* of his followers. Like the other whites in the area, Harrison was rather dismayed when the Shawnee leader showed up at Vincennes with several hundred men. The group waiting on the porch at Grouseland must have given a small sigh of relief when Tecumseh finally came into sight on the morning of August 15: The Shawnee leader had left most of his warriors in camp and was accompanied by only a dozen or so advisers and bodyguards. The Shawnee had left their rifles in camp, too, although they still carried their knives, war clubs, and tomahawks.

From the first moment, Tecumseh dominated the meeting. Instead of coming to the porch so that Harrison could welcome him into the mansion, he halted thirty or forty yards from the house. He told one of Harrison's interpreters that he would prefer to meet outdoors. Harrison politely agreed, but he had lost the advantage that lay in controlling the setting of the council. The governor ordered his slaves to set up chairs in the shade of grape arbors in the garden. There Harrison invited the Shawnee to sit, saying that the Indians' Great White Father in Washington (the president) wanted them to be comfortable.

Once again, however, Tecumseh threw the governor off guard. According to several witnesses who later recorded their versions of the encounter, Tecumseh pointed dramatically upward and declared, "My father? The Great Spirit is my father—the earth is my mother—and on her bosom I will recline." With these words Tecumseh and his men settled on the ground, leaving the whites to stand or sit awkwardly around them. With a few shrewd moves Tecumseh had shown Harrison that he was not a simple "savage" who could easily be manipulated.

Tecumseh continued to unsettle the white men. He spoke first, and he spoke for a long time—as long as two hours, according to one account. Harrison later said that the Shawnee had spoken "at unfortunate length."

Tecumseh's long opening speech was a history lesson—the history of white settlement in North America from the Native Americans' point of view. He recounted the sad story of relations between the Indians and the whites. The whites, said Tecumseh, had treated the tribes unjustly and with great cruelty. He listed many occasions when white people had betrayed, cheated, attacked, or slaughtered Indians. His listeners knew that the charges were founded in fact. As Harrison later wrote to his superiors at the U.S. War Department, "Every instance of injustice and injury which have been committed by our citizens upon the Indians from the commencement of the revolutionary war (There are unfortunately too many of them) was brought forward and exaggerated."

Tecumseh then moved on to the subject of treaties, the agreements by which the English, and later the Americans, had acquired land from the Native Americans. He told how the whites had made one treaty after another with various Indian leaders, each time promising to settle the land only up to the treaty line and no farther, each time breaking their promise. Fifteen years ago, Tecumseh reminded his audience, the U.S. government had won huge tracts of Indian land under the Treaty of Greenville. That treaty had drawn a border between Indian lands and non-Indian lands; the whites had agreed never to cross the border, but they did so nonetheless, and in ever greater numbers. Settlers were pushing north and west into the Indian territory between the Ohio River and the Great Lakes, making it impossible for the Native Americans to hunt and live there. "You are continually driving the red people [and will] at last drive them into the great lake where they can't either stand or work," said Tecumseh. The final outrage had occurred just one year ago. Harrison had persuaded chieftains of some tribes to sign an agreement called the Treaty of Fort Wayne. Under this treaty the Indians gave up still more land—land that the Treaty of Greenville had stipulated as

NATIVE AMERICANS AND THE ART OF SPEECHMAKING

Oratory, or the art of making effective speeches, was highly valued by the Shawnee and other Native Americans. Because the Indians had not established a phonetic writing system with an alphabet, the spoken word was of great importance in their cultures, and the ability to persuade or inspire others through speeches was one of the characteristics of a good leader. "Those who could hold the rapt attention of a village or nation for hours as they spoke of serious matters were counted as great men," writes historian Bil Gilbert. Tecumseh had earned something of a reputation as an orator, and at Grouseland he showed why.

Unfortunately, Tecumseh's exact words did not survive. Apparently Tecumseh could speak some English, although reports by those who knew him vary on this matter as on many others. He is said to have conversed in English with many white people during his adult life. His speeches, however, were in the Shawnee language. Interpreters relayed his words to white audiences, who sometimes wrote them down or summarized them. The only existing records of Tecumseh's orations at Grouseland are accounts written later by Harrison himself and a few of the other Americans who were present. These accounts are based on memory and some notes made by one of Harrison's interpreters.

Quotations from Tecumseh sometimes seem to echo the rhythm and vocabulary of educated white speakers of the 18th and early 19th centuries, suggesting that those who recorded Tecumseh's speeches sometimes used forms of speech that seemed familiar and appropriate to them. We have no way of knowing how closely these matched Tecumseh's actual utterances. However, on several occasions during Tecumseh's lifetime, two or more listeners took simultaneous notes on speeches that he delivered. By comparing these notes, looking for phrases and expressions that appear in more than one version, scholars have been able to establish at least some of what Tecumseh really said.

theirs forever. The history of treaties, said Tecumseh scornfully, was a history of broken vows.

Now Tecumseh came to the heart of his message. He declared that the Treaty of Fort Wayne was no good and must be set aside. He and his followers would never accept it, because the greedy, cowardly, or confused chiefs who signed the treaty the year before had had no right to give away the land.

Here Tecumseh touched on an essential difference that made it almost impossible for Native Americans and whites of European descent to understand each other: their dramatically distinct beliefs about land ownership. To the Europeans who settled North America and their descendants who became American citizens after the Revolution, every square inch of land existed to be owned, bought, and sold. Not only did they believe that it was possible for an individual to own land, but doing so was one of their most cherished goals. A man's place in society was defined, in part, by whether he owned land and, if so, by how much land he owned. Therefore it seemed natural and right to white people to believe that Indian chieftains were the owners of the land on which their tribes lived, and that those chieftains could dispose of the land as they wished—for example, by selling it to the whites.

The Native Americans, however, did not parcel land out into individually owned tracts. In fact, the concept of individual land ownership was not part of their cultures. Different tribes or bands might negotiate or go to war over the right to hunt or live in certain territories, but they did not think that they *owned* those territories. Their claim on the land existed only as long as they lived on it. Native Americans "belonged" to the land as much as it "belonged" to them. No one—not even a chief or a council of chiefs—could sell or give away something that belonged to no one. In short, Indians and whites viewed the world in ways that were not just different but opposite. Some modern scholars of American and Native American history believe that this fundamental difference in worldview doomed the two peoples to a conflict that could not end until one had completely overcome the other.

Tecumseh continued to speak. He told Harrison that he and his brother the Prophet were working to ensure against more treaties like Greenville or Fort Wayne. As Harrison later wrote to the War Department, the brothers had "organized a combination of all the Indian tribes in this quarter to put a stop to the encroachments of the white people and to establish a principle that the lands should be considered common property and none sold without the consent of all."

Next came Tecumseh's most startling and threatening announcement: If the American government wanted peace along the frontier, it must cancel the Treaty of Fort Wayne. The Shawnee leader looked at Harrison and said with great emphasis, "I now wish you to listen to me. If you do not [cancel the treaty] it will appear as if you wished me to kill all the chiefs that sold you this land. I tell you so because I am authorized by all the tribes to do so. I am the head of them all."

Tecumseh then pointed at Winamac, the Potawatomi chieftain, and declared him a traitor who had tricked other chieftains into signing the treaty that cheated the Indians out of their land. He began yelling at Winamac in Shawnee, speaking so rapidly and violently that the interpreters could not—or were afraid to—translate what he was saying. Alarmed, Winamac pulled a gun from his clothes and began loading it. Some of the white onlookers grabbed him and hustled him away.

Harrison tried to ease the tension by telling Tecumseh that the United States had always treated the Indians fairly. "You are a liar," Tecumseh spat in Shawnee. An army officer who understood Shawnee feared that violence was about to break out. He ordered the soldiers to step forward and cock their rifles. When they did so, Tecumseh's bodyguards leaped to their feet, brandishing their tomahawks. Harrison drew his sword; by now he and Tecumseh were on their feet, glaring at one another. After a long moment, Harrison ordered the soldiers to lower their rifles. Then he turned and marched away from the council site, followed by the other members of the American delegation.

By the next morning, tempers on both sides had cooled. Tecumseh and Harrison met again. They held several discussions in the days that followed, but Tecumseh would not budge from his position: The boundary established by the Treaty of Greenville must continue to hold, and the Treaty of Fort Wayne was not valid. The United States should not expect to occupy the lands it had unfairly gained under the Treaty of Fort Wayne. If the government tried to survey or settle those lands, violence would result.

Tecumseh was not the only voice of the Native Americans. Representatives of the Kickapoo, Wyandot, Potawatomi, Ottawa, and Winnebago nations had accompanied Tecumseh to Vincennes, and they too spoke to Harrison. They told him that many people in their nations agreed with Tecumseh and would support him.

A tense moment between Shawnee war leader Tecumseh and William Henry Harrison, governor of the Indiana Territory. For years these two men fought each other to determine the fate of the Old Northwest. *(Indiana Historical Society, negative C3798)*

The conference ended on August 21. Harrison repeated an earlier invitation that Tecumseh and the Prophet go to Washington and meet with President Madison. Harrison felt that the trip east would impress the Shawnee leaders with the might of the U.S. government and make them realize that it was useless to keep resisting the American advance. Tecumseh, however, showed no interest in journeying to the white man's capital. Instead, he advised Harrison to send to Washington the speeches that he and the other Indians had made. He repeated that no further dealings could be considered until the U.S. government declared the Treaty of Fort Wayne invalid. And he told Harrison to stay out of Indian politics and stop trying to set one tribe against another.

Harrison asked how, if the Treaty of Fort Wayne were cancelled, the tribes would receive their annuities—the annual sums that the government had agreed to pay them under the terms of the treaty. Tecumseh's response contained a warning:

> Brother. When you speak to me of annuities I look at the land, and pity the women and children. I am authorized to say that they will not receive them. Brother. They want to save that piece of land. We do not wish you to take it. It is small enough for our purposes. If you do take it you must blame yourself as the cause of trouble between us and the Tribes who sold it to you. I want the present boundary line to continue. Should you cross it, I assure you it will be productive of bad consequences.

The governor said he would send Tecumseh's words to President Madison in Washington. He added, however, that they would not change things. In an account written many years later, Harrison claimed that Tecumseh then looked at him sadly and replied, "[The president] is so far off he will not be injured by the war; he may sit still in his town and drink his wine, whilst you and I will have to fight it out."

That afternoon Tecumseh left Vincennes. He and Harrison would meet again. And as Tecumseh had predicted, they would fight it out.

NOTES

p. 1 "well prepared . . ." and "one of the finest looking men . . ." Quoted in Allan W. Eckert, *A Sorrow in Our Heart: The Life of Tecumseh* (New York: Bantam Books, 1992), p. 761.

p. 4 "My father? . . ." Quoted in Bil Gilbert, *God Gave Us This Country* (New York: Atheneum, 1989), p. 257.

p. 5 "at unfortunate length." Quoted in Gilbert, p. 257.

p. 5 "Every instance of injustice . . ." Quoted in Eckert, p. 761.

p. 5 "You are continually driving . . ." Quoted in Gilbert, p. 257.

p. 6 "Those who could hold . . ." Gilbert, p. 85.

p. 8 "organized a combination . . ." Quoted in R. David Edmunds, *Tecumseh and the Quest for Indian Leadership* (Boston: Little, Brown, 1984), p. 132.

p. 8 "I now wish you . . ." Quoted in Gilbert, p. 258.

p. 10 "Brother. When you speak . . ." Quoted in Edmunds, p. 134.

p. 10 "[The president] is so far off . . ." Quoted in Edmunds, p. 134.

2 WAR ALONG THE FRONTIER

B etween the end of the American Revolution in 1783 and the beginning of the War of 1812, a simmering crisis burst into flames on the western frontier of U.S. settlement. It involved the land north of the Ohio River, the area that Americans would come to call the Old Northwest: a 250,000-square-mile wilderness that included the present-day states of Ohio, Indiana, Illinois, Michigan, and Wisconsin. In this territory warfare raged between the Native Americans of the region and the land-hungry white settlers who had begun flooding into the Old Northwest in the 1770s.

The Native Americans tried repeatedly to win assurances from the U.S. government that the land north of the Ohio River would remain Indian land forever. When negotiation failed, they turned to war. The Indian wars of the Old Northwest Territory included some of the most vicious fighting between whites and Native Americans since the Spanish onquest of Peru. Each side committed atrocities against the other. As time went on, the views of leaders on each side grew more extreme. Compromise, it seemed, was impossible. One side or the other must emerge victorious.

One of the most remarkable features of this struggle was that the Native American peoples of the Old Northwest tried several times to set aside their long-standing feuds and mutual mistrust to form a single organized force. Such a unified force, some Indian leaders believed, would be more effective against the whites than many scattered small groups. The gifted and charismatic Tecumseh led the most spirited of these attempts. Yet Tecumseh wanted to do more than keep American settlers out of Indian land. He also dreamed of returning the Native Americans of the Ohio River valley to their traditional way of life, a way of life that had been eroded by contact with the whites and their culture.

Ironically, in his quest to restore Native American tradition, Tecumseh brought something new to the North American Indians: the idea to unite against a common enemy and in pursuit of a common goal. In other words, he tried to do with the Indian tribes of the Old Northwest what colonial patriots like John Adams and George Washington had done with the colonies before the American Revolution. Historian Harvey Lewis Carter has even suggested that Tecumseh got the idea of forming a confederacy, or group of nations joined under a common government, from observing the United States government. Carter writes, "Perhaps [Tecumseh] borrowed the idea of the 'united states' or 'seventeen fires' as the Indians called them, for white leaders pointed out the strength of such a combination." It is also likely that Tecumseh was inspired by other Indian unions, such as the Iroquois Confederacy. Whatever the immediate source of Tecumseh's vision of Indian unity, the seeds of his struggle were planted when Europeans established their first small colonies on the Atlantic coast of North America.

When Europeans arrived in North America, about sixty Native American tribes lived in the eastern part of the continent, the region bounded by the St. Lawrence River valley and the Great Lakes in the north, the Gulf of Mexico in the south, the Atlantic Ocean in the east, and the Mississippi River in the west. Most of this immense landscape was woodland. A vast shadowy forest carpeted range after range of low but rugged mountains that were cut by winding valleys and broken up here and there by plains. Only in the west, where the land flattened out as it approached the Mississippi, did the thick forest give way to stretches of open prairie.

The Indians who lived in the eastern woodlands followed ways of life that they had developed over centuries. These ways of life were well suited to the world in which they lived because the

Native Americans adapted their economy and habits to the environment rather than changing the environment to suit the needs of an economic or social system. They did not build big cities that would consume resources, such as firewood and food, from a large area. Few Indian communities were larger than several thousand people, and most were considerably smaller. A tribe might occupy dozens or even hundreds of communities spread over a large area.

Indian settlements were rarely permanent. Among many tribes it was common for an entire community to move to a new village—or return to an old one—after a few years. This movement gave the land and its wildlife a chance to recover from use. The Indians traveled through the forest on narrow trails and used canoes to navigate the network of lakes, streams, and rivers that spans eastern North America. Men hunted and fished; women tended gardens and fields in the rich soil of flat bottomlands along streams, growing beans, pumpkins, squash, and—except in the northern part of the region—corn, or maize. This way of life

An 1820 painting of a temporary Shawnee forest camp. The "2" near the pole-and-bark shelter indicates a baby's hammock. The figure marked "3" is a woman grinding corn in a hollow log. *(Tulane University Art Collection)*

sustained the Native American population in harmony with the environment, and it had changed little for hundreds of years.

Although all of the Indians of the eastern woodlands followed a similar way of life, they belonged to many distinct tribes, or nations. Anthropologists, scientists who study human societies, have grouped the tribes into large categories based on relationships between either the languages or the tools and artifacts of the various Indian nations. They call these categories language groups and culture groups. Even within the same language or culture group, however, each Native American nation or tribe had its own characteristics and identity.

Tecumseh's people, the Shawnee, were part of the large family called the Algonquian language group. The name "Shawnee" comes from the Algonquian word *sawanwa*, which means "person of the south." Yet the Shawnee are not a particularly southern people. In fact, their history is a sprawling one that wanders through all of eastern North America, from north of the Great Lakes to Florida's Swanee River, which bears their name.

The early history of the Shawnee is something of a mystery. Scholars have peered into the past, studying legends and myths, vocabulary words, and artifacts for clues about the origins of the Shawnee. Many researchers believe that the Shawnee were originally part of a large group known to anthropologists as the Fort Ancient Aspect people. The Fort Ancient culture flourished in the Ohio River valley of western West Virginia, southern Ohio and Indiana, and northern Kentucky between A.D. 1200 and 1600. The Fort Ancient culture group was closely related to the large and influential Mississippian culture group, a family of peoples who lived along the Mississippi and in the Southeast. At the beginning of the 17th century the Fort Ancient culture broke up, possibly because of the new and deadly diseases that traveled through the Native American population with lightning speed after being introduced to the continent by the first European explorers and traders. The Shawnee, according to one interpretation of history, were one of the Fort Ancient peoples to spread out across eastern North America from their Ohio River homeland.

Native American groups often warred against one another, as in this battle between Sac and Ojibwa forces on Lake Superior. Tecumseh was one of several Indian leaders who urged them to stop fighting each other and unite against their common enemy. *(Library of Congress)*

A rival school of thought, however, links the Shawnee with the Ojibwa* and other Native American peoples of the northern Great Lakes region. Like the Ojibwa, the Shawnee built dome-shaped dwellings, pole frameworks covered with broad strips of bark. Furthermore, some Shawnee words and traditions are very similar to those of the Ojibwa. This has led some researchers to believe that the Shawnee originated in the north, possibly even in southern Canada. To escape pressure from the powerful and aggressive Ojibwa, the Shawnee migrated south.

It is clear that groups of Shawnee passed through a number of places from the Great Lakes region to Florida, Georgia, and the Carolinas—and that they were often at war with other tribes.

---

*Historically the term Chippewa has been used for this group in the United States and Ojibwa in Canada. Recently many have began using the term Anishinabe, meaning "first people."

When Europeans began exploring North America, they learned from their Indian contacts of "a roving, troublesome people" in the interior. These nomadic troublemakers were the Shawnee.

We may never know the history of the Shawnee before about 1650; however, we do know that their history from that time on was one of constant movement, migration, and fragmentation. For one reason or another, the Shawnee had become a displaced people looking for a new homeland. They attempted to settle in the northern Ohio River valley in the late 17th century but were thwarted by regional turbulence. In the 1680s the Iroquois Confederacy, a group of tribes from the St. Lawrence River valley and northern New York, was making war on the tribes of the eastern Ohio River. The Huron tribe of Canada was also active in the area, as were the French and English traders who were busy introducing the fur trade. The Shawnee became embroiled in the fighting. In 1683 they allied themselves with the Miami, an Ohio tribe battling the invading Iroquois. Although the Shawnee earned the friendship of the Miami, turmoil in the region continued.

Unable to carve out a territory of their own in all this confusion, the Shawnee split into bands that moved off in various directions. They went south to Georgia, west to Illinois, north to Michigan, and east to western Virginia and Pennsylvania. Many of these bands soon ran into trouble. The Chickasaw and Creek resisted the Shawnees' attempt to settle in the Southeast. The Iroquois Confederacy attacked those who had gone to Michigan. The Shawnee in Illinois did not find the prairie to their liking. Around 1707 many of the far-flung Shawnee began migrating to Pennsylvania to join their kinfolk who had settled there.

Pennsylvania, in turn, did not provide a satisfactory homeland. The colony's British authorities treated the Shawnee as subjects of the Iroquois Confederacy, which angered and humiliated the Shawnee. In addition, the Pennsylvania colony soon acquired a reputation for good farmland as well as for religious liberty. As a result, more and more Europeans were coming to the colony. The inrush of new settlers kept pushing the Shawnee off their land, and it was not long before the Shawnee and the whites were at odds.

A new stage in Shawnee history began around 1725. The tribes of the Iroquois Confederacy were now confining their activities to their own homeland, and the Miami invited the Shawnee to settle in Miami territory. Widely dispersed bands of Shawnee began moving from all directions toward the Ohio valley. By mid-century more Shawnee were living on the north bank of the Ohio River than had ever lived in one place before. Although they did not settle south of the river, they regularly hunted there, ranging far into Kentucky and Tennessee.

The wanderings of the Shawnee had given the tribe certain qualities. The Shawnee had had more contact with other tribes than most eastern Indians did. They were accustomed to meeting, communicating, and negotiating with the chieftains and warriors of many peoples—skills that Tecumseh would demonstrate to their fullest. The Shawnee had also become brilliant fighters. Although they were fewer in number than many tribes, they were skilled in woodcraft and warfare. Other tribes often used Shawnee warriors as mercenaries, or soldiers for hire. The Shawnee made such an impression on French explorer René-Robert Cavelier de La Salle that he called them "the best, finest, most intelligent and most skilled warriors in America." La Salle took two Shawnee to France with him to show Europeans just how admirable Native Americans could be.

As the Shawnee converged on Ohio, they established settlements along the northern tributaries of the Ohio River, especially the Scioto, Mad, Muskingum, and Miami rivers. Their neighbors to the northwest were the Miami. Farther west lived the Potawatomi, Kickapoo, and Chippewa. The Wyandot, descendants of the Huron, lived to the north. The Ohio valley was also home to groups of Delaware who had moved west from Pennsylvania and of Cherokee who had moved north from Tennessee. Finally there were the Mingo, a term that applied to groups of Iroquois-speaking peoples who did not belong to the Iroquois Confederacy. In the mid-18th century these tribes lived together fairly harmoniously, on the whole. In the years to come, their destinies would be intertwined—in part through the deeds of Tecumseh and his brother, the Shawnee Prophet.

While the Shawnee were making a homeland for themselves in the Ohio valley, a battle was brewing for control of the Old Northwest. The battle was not between the Indians and the whites—at least not yet. At this time it was between the French and the British. These two powers, seemingly always at war or on the verge of it in Europe, were vying for control of the fur trade in the Old Northwest. For years scouts and traders had been crossing the Appalachian Mountains or working their way south from the Great Lakes to make deals with the Indians. In exchange for the furs of beaver and other animals they offered trade goods such as steel knives, iron skillets, mirrors, blankets, and manufactured cloth.

At first the Indians had regarded trade items as curiosities and novelties—good to have, but not necessary. Before long, however, they began to grow dependent on trade goods, especially on the guns and liquor that swiftly became the most prized trade items. Both firearms and alcohol were new to indigenous America. Liquor's effects were particularly devastating on individuals, families, and communities. As early as 1701, some Shawnee elders recognized the evils of alcoholism and asked the British to ban the trade in liquor. The trade continued, however, because there were always whites willing to make and sell alcohol and Indians willing to buy it.

Trade in general—not just the trade in alcohol—quickly changed entire cultures. People who had formerly turned to the land to satisfy all their own needs now devoted much of their energy to obtaining furs for the white traders. The men hunted beaver, mink, marten, and fox; the women cleaned and prepared the pelts. These activities took time that would previously have been spent securing food for the tribe and making deerskin clothing. As trade took hold, some families and villages began to rely on the flour, other foods, ready-made garments, or blankets and cloth that they received from the whites. In addition, the Indians were drawn into the rivalry between French and British traders. Representatives of the rival European powers alternated between trying to win the support of the Indian tribes through gifts and flattery and punishing them for supporting the wrong side.

The fur trade was not the only thing that was entering the Old Northwest. Behind the traders came settlers: at first just a few forts and woodsmen, then a handful of families, and then more and more farms and settlements. In this respect, the French and British attitudes toward settlement of the interior of North America were quite different. The French did not want to occupy the interior. They wanted only to trade there and to build forts that would prevent another European power from claiming the region. The British, on the other hand, were as interested in long-term settlement as in the fur trade—maybe more interested. The Delaware and the Shawnee, who had lived in Britain's Atlantic colonies, understood better than other tribes that once settlement began it

Whites entering the Northwest often lived side by side with Indians. In the early years, their interactions included peaceful trade, friendship, and intermarriage. *(Library of Congress)*

would be relentless. Native Americans very often lived in harmony and even established friendships with explorers, scouts, traders, and the other whites who first penetrated the fringes of their territories. Large-scale permanent settlement, however, was a different matter. Indian territory with a few whites living and working around its edges would become white territory—and what would become of the Indians? The idea of resistance to further settlement, of a boundary beyond which the land would forever belong only to the tribes, began to take shape in the minds of some Native Americans.

The Shawnee were quick to see the changes that Europeans were bringing to the Ohio valley. They played the French against the British, always trying to get the best deal they could, not hesitating to switch sides when doing so was to their advantage. To the British, the Iroquois criticized the Shawnee, calling them a people "remarked for their deceit and perfidy, paying little or no regard to their word and most solemn engagements"—but the Iroquois Confederacy had a long history of conflict with the Shawnee. The confederacy was essentially competing against the Shawnee for sole control of British dealings with the Indians; therefore, it would scarcely have been in the confederacy's interest to sing the virtues of the Shawnee. Nevertheless, the Shawnees' years as wanderers had apparently sharpened their survival skills and made them shrewd bargainers. And it may be that in forming relationships with both sides the Shawnee hoped to remain neutral in a conflict that was not of their making.

In the decades before Tecumseh's birth, the Shawnee made short-lived alliances with both the French and the British. In 1739 some Shawnee mercenaries were part of a French expedition against the southern Chickasaw tribe, which was allied with the British. A Shawnee war party also attacked another British ally, the Catawba tribe of South Carolina. Yet in the 1740s the Shawnee attacked a French post on the Wabash River, allowed British agents to enter their villages, and tried to persuade the Miami to give up their alliance with the French. This angered the French, who sent raiding parties into the Ohio valley to destroy British trading posts and kill or drive out British traders. In 1750 a Shawnee village was destroyed by one of these French raiding parties. The Shawnee appealed to Pennsylvania's colonial legislature for help but received none.

All this while, the confrontation between the French and the British was getting closer. The Shawnee saw that French military and trading power was on the rise throughout the Old Northwest, so they bet on the French. In 1754, when war broke out between the British and French, the Shawnee were French allies.

The French and Indian War, as the British colonists in North America called it, was part of a larger conflict between the two powers in Europe, known there as the Seven Years' War. The Shawnee were fairly active in the early years of the war. Shawnee warriors joined French troops and warriors from other tribes to inflict a crushing defeat on a British force under General Edward Braddock in July of 1755. Emboldened by this victory, the Shawnee and other tribes of the Old Northwest began attacking British settlements in western Pennsylvania and Virginia.

The war went slowly on, and slowly the tide turned. The French in Canada were desperately undersupplied, and they could provide little in the way of supplies to their Indian allies. By 1757 the Shawnee of eastern Ohio were running low on ammunition. They were running low on food, too, because the war had taken the men away from their hunting and had disrupted trade. The British, on the other hand, were building more forts and were advancing steadily against the French. In 1758 they captured Fort Duquesne, a French outpost on the present-day site of Pittsburgh. Seeing which way the wind was blowing, some Shawnee switched sides. They helped the British in several campaigns, asking in return that the British keep their settlers from crossing the Appalachian Mountains.

The alliance between the Shawnee and the British soon began to crack. The British rebuilt Fort Duquesne, calling it Fort Pitt. They also opened the Forbes Road, a trail through the wilderness from Philadelphia to Fort Pitt. Although the British claimed that they had made the Forbes Road for military supply wagons, some

Indians saw the trail as a broad, inviting highway that would draw settlers west to the headwaters of the Ohio River. It began to seem that the British might not withdraw to the east side of the Appalachians after beating the French.

The Indians were even more concerned about new rules that governed the British traders. Lord Jeffrey Amherst, commander in chief of British forces in North America, disliked Indians and was determined to put to an end to the widely accepted practice of giving gifts of food and ammunition to friendly chiefs. He did not realize that the exchange of gifts was a vital part of Native American culture and had become firmly entrenched in frontier diplomacy. To make matters worse, he reduced the number of traders who would be allowed to do business with the Indians and declared that trade could take place only at licensed British trading posts, not in Indian villages as had often been the case in the past. Amherst's actions created great bitterness among the Old Northwest Indians, who now regarded the British as stingy and heartless.

Another issue was driving a wedge between the British and the Indians. British colonial authorities demanded that the Indians hand over all their white "captives." The Shawnee agreed that if any of the white people who were living among them wanted to return to white society, they could do so. Some whites, however, chose to stay with the Indians. The Shawnee villages contained a number of white men and women who had married Shawnee and were raising interracial families. In 1762, under increasing pressure from the British, the Shawnee did take all of the whites, both willing and unwilling, to British frontier posts. To the dismay of the British, some of the returned "captives" promptly escaped and disappeared into the woods—even though the British had had them guarded by soldiers. The escapees soon made their way back to their Shawnee homes, where they were warmly welcomed.

During the final years of the French and Indian War, the Shawnee saw their fears about the Forbes Road justified. Settlers were clearing lots and building cabins at the western end of the road. Near Fort Pitt they had established the community of Pitts-

INDIANS AND THEIR CAPTIVES

The subject of whites who were taken captive by Native Americans is a complex one, and it is often impossible to sort out fact from legend and hearsay. Since the earliest days of European settlement in North America, white men, women, and children lived in Indian communities. Most were taken by force, but some joined the Indians voluntarily. And of those who were captured or kidnapped against their will, a fair number came to prefer Indian life to life in the white settlements. One such person was Mary Jemison, who was captured as a young girl in Pennsylvania. After fifty years of marriage to a Seneca warrior, she reported that her life with the Indians had been a happy one. She said that her husband "uniformly treated me with tenderness and never offered an insult."

One way that whites became members of Indian families and tribes was through adoption. It had long been common among the Shawnee and other woodland tribes to adopt prisoners of war into their families to replace relatives who had died. After white people appeared on the scene, the Shawnee continued this practice, adopting Europeans and later Americans as readily as they adopted Native Americans from other tribes.

Undoubtedly many white captives regarded their time with the Indians as a nightmare and longed to return to their homes, but there are many well-founded accounts of "captives" who refused to be rescued. Some, when forcibly returned to white "civilization," fled back to the Indians. Yet Europeans refused to acknowledge this fact, even among themselves, for it upset their belief in their superiority over the "savages." If Europeans were better than Indians, as most Europeans firmly believed, than how could any white person choose the Indian way of life? European authorities, therefore, glossed over or ignored the existence of these renegades and insisted that all whites living among the Indians were suffering horrible fates and must be returned.

The issue of Indian captives would not go away. After the French and Indian War, the Shawnee and other tribes would continue to take white captives, and white people from the settlements would continue to "go native." By the time Tecumseh was growing up, some fifty or sixty whites lived among the Shawnee in his part of Ohio.

One captive became an important Shawnee leader. His name was Marmaduke van Swearingen, and he was seventeen years old when a Shawnee war party captured him during a raid in western Virginia. The Shawnee adopted him into the tribe, calling him Blue Jacket after the garment he had been wearing when he was captured. Blue Jacket was a willing convert to the Shawnee way of life. Although he had many opportunities to return to white civilization, he took none of them. Instead he rose to a position of power and leadership among the Shawnee, who had no racial prejudice and regarded him as one of them. As a chieftain, Blue Jacket would be one of Tecumseh's staunchest friends and supporters.

Of course, not all white captives were happy among the Indians, and some of them encountered terrible fates. In some cases the Indians simply turned captives loose in the woods, to live or die by chance. Other captives became prisoners or slaves. And yet other captives were killed. The Shawnee were generally kind to captive women and children. But if they captured a white man who had made war on Indians, they were likely to execute him, perhaps after prolonged torture. A common method of execution was to mutilate the prisoner, then tie him to a stake and burn him slowly. As friction between Indians and settlers increased during the second half of the 18th century, such tragedies became more common.

Stories of people taken by Indians have fascinated Americans since the earliest days of settlement. Many Indian captivity narratives appeared in print during the 18th and 19th centuries. Accounts of some of the better-documented captivities have been collected in Alice Dickinson's *Taken by Indians: True Tales of Captivity* (New York: Franklin Watts, 1976), James Levernier and Kathryn Derounian-Stodola's *The Indian Captivity Narrative* (New York: Macmillan, 1993), and Richard Van-DerBeets's *Held Captive by Indians: Selected Narratives, 1642–1836* (Knoxville: University of Tennessee Press, revised edition, 1994).

burgh. Even worse were the frontiersmen who ranged west into Kentucky and Ohio on extended hunting trips. The Indians called these roving hunters Long Knives and did not hesitate to kill them. The Long Knives were deep in Indian country, slaughtering game to which they had no right.

The Shawnee were not the only tribe feeling hostile toward the British. To the north the Ottawa were outraged by the British refusal to provide weapons and supplies. Pontiac, an Ottawa chieftain, led his tribe and its allies in a revolt against Detroit and other British posts around the Great Lakes. In June of 1763 the Ohio valley Shawnee and Delaware joined Pontiac's Rebellion. For a few wild weeks they vented their wrath on the frontier settlements of western Pennsylvania and Virginia, burning settlers' cabins and taking their scalps. They even tried to seize Fort Pitt, but that attempt failed. In early August British troops defeated Pontiac's forces at a place called Bushy Run, not far from Fort Pitt. The Shawnee retreated into Ohio.

Because the Ottawa and their allies had taken the French side in the French and Indian War, Pontiac had hoped that the French in North America would help the Indians in their battles. The French, however, were now being beaten right and left by the British and, therefore, prudently refused to get involved in new conflicts. Without aid or ammunition from the French, Pontiac's Rebellion sputtered to a halt. In November the last of Pontiac's warriors abandoned their fruitless siege of Detroit. Pontiac's Rebellion was over. It had done little except to increase white settlers' fear of and hostility toward the Indians. Yet the rebellion was significant in one way: It had united warriors from several Indian nations against a common enemy. People of many tribes would remember Pontiac and how he had inspired them to work together toward a goal that no tribe could win alone. Forty years later Tecumseh would set out to do the same thing on a much larger scale.

The year 1763 brought much more than the end of Pontiac's Rebellion. It also brought the end of the French and Indian War in North America and the Seven Years' War in Europe. Britain was the victor, and one of its prizes was France's North American territories. The French were gone from the Old Northwest. No longer would the Shawnee be able to play one power against the other.

The British sent troops into the Old Northwest to reclaim, by force if necessary, all white prisoners held by the Shawnee and the Delaware. However, the British also responded to the Indians' concerns about encroaching white settlement on what was still Native American land. In the Proclamation of 1763, signed by King George III of England, the British agreed that the summit of the Appalachian Mountains was the western frontier of colonial settlement. Although the British would maintain military forts and trading posts west of the mountains, no white settlers would be allowed to cross the mountains, and those who had already crossed were ordered to move back east.

The Proclamation of 1763 had about as much effect as King Canute's legendary attempt to hold back the rising ocean tide. British troops on the Forbes Road did stop some settlers who were headed west. The British even forcibly removed some of the settlers who had already established themselves on the Indian side of the line. But they could not hold back the human tide. Land-hungry people in the colonies believed that they had a right to settle wherever they wanted. John Amberson, a settler in the Ohio country, expressed that belief when he wrote a few years later, "I do certify that all mankind . . . have an undoubted right to pass into every vacant country." The Ohio country was not vacant, of course, but to most settlers the Indians simply did not count. Indians were spread thinly across the land and did not use the land in the way that white farmers would use it. Many whites, therefore, felt that the Indians did not really need the land and had no right to object to settlement.

The Proclamation of 1763, and the troops that were supposed to back it up, simply could not keep people from finding their way across the boundary line. Frontiersmen ignored the proclamation and continued to build homes in western Pennsylvania and West Virginia. And in truth the British government was divided on the issue of western settlement. Some factions in the government

EASTERN NORTH AMERICA, 1765

Lake Superior
SIOUX
Mississippi R.
WINNEBAGO
Fort Michilimackinac
Lake Michigan
Lake Huron
OJIBWA
OTTAWA
SAUK
FOX
POTAWATOMI
WYANDOT
Detroit
Lake Erie
Lake Ontario
Fort Stanwix
IROQUOIS
MASSACHU-SETTS
NEW HAMP.
NEW YORK
MASS.
Boston
CONN.
RHODE ISLAND
IOWA
ILLINOIS
KICKAPOO
MIAMI
DELAWARE
SHAWNEES
Fort Pitt
PENNSYLVANIA
New York
Philadelphia
NEW JERSEY
Baltimore
DELAWARE
MARYLAND
Missouri R.
St. Louis
Vincennes
Ohio R.
VIRGINIA
Williamsburg
OSAGE
Tennessee R.
Mississippi R.
CHICKASAW
CHEROKEE
Appalachian
NORTH CAROLINA
SOUTH CAROLINA
Charleston
Atlantic Ocean
N
CREEK
GEORGIA
CHOCTAW
SEMINOLE
New Orleans
Gulf of Mexico

——— Proclamation of 1763 line
☐ Area of thirteen colonies
——— Colonial borders
0   150   300 miles
0   150 300 kilometers

At the end of the French and Indian War, settlers from the British colonies on the coast were poised to cross the Proclamation of 1763 boundary line into territory inhabited by a dozen or more Indian tribes.

wanted to keep the colonists confined to the eastern side of the mountains, where they could more easily be overseen, controlled—and taxed. Other factions felt that Britain should extend its colonial holdings into the interior and that the best way to do so was by allowing settlement. Besides, argued some authorities in Britain, colonists were going to settle on the frontier with or without official permission. It would be best if these settlers remained under British rule. Before long the British authorities were tinkering with the proclamation, tugging at the boundary line, pulling it westward.

The biggest "adjustment" came in 1768, when the British and the Iroquois Confederacy made a deal called the Treaty of Fort Stanwix. Under this treaty the Iroquois sold southwestern New York, western Pennsylvania, and parts of West Virginia, Kentucky, and Tennessee to the British. There were just a few problems with the treaty: Not only did the Iroquois Confederacy not own these lands, the tribes of the confederacy did not even live in some of them. And the tribes that *did* live or hunt there, including the Shawnee, rejected the Iroquois claim to overlordship. In their opinion, the Iroquois nations of New York had no right to sell other tribes' land to the whites. Yet the British, who had long accepted the Iroquois Confederacy's claim to supremacy over the other Indians of eastern North America, felt that they had made a solid bargain. The stage was set for strife.

NOTES

p. 13   "Perhaps [Tecumseh] borrowed . . ." Harvey Lewis Carter, *The Life and Times of Little Turtle* (Urbana and Chicago: University of Illinois Press, 1987), p. 191.

p. 17   "a roving, troublesome people." Bil Gilbert, *God Gave Us This Country* (New York: Atheneum, 1989), p. 39.

p. 18   "the best, finest . . ." Quoted in Terrance Dolan, *The Shawnee Indians* (New York: Chelsea House, 1996), p. 41.

p. 21   "remarked for their deceit . . ." Quoted in Gilbert, p. 47.

p. 24   "uniformly treated me . . ." Quoted in Gilbert, p. 82.

p. 27   "I do certify . . ." Quoted in Sanford Wexler, *Westward Expansion: An Eyewitness History* (New York: Facts On File, 1991), p. 29.

THE PANTHER CROSSES THE SKY

The Treaty of Fort Stanwix was not the only event of 1768 that would change Shawnee history. That year a baby named Tecumseh was born in southern Ohio. He would have an enormous impact not only on the Native Americans of the Old Northwest but on the westward growth of the United States.

Tecumseh's father, Puckeshinwa, was destined to be a warrior, and so was Tecumseh. In Shawnee culture, all tribe members belonged to one of five broad groups. Anthropologists call these groups septs. Each sept traditionally provided certain services to the tribe as a whole, and each community contained people of various septs. The Pekowi sept was responsible for performing rituals. The Mekoche sept provided healers. The Chalahkatha and Thawikila septs handled politics, diplomacy, and leadership; these two septs traditionally produced each community's peace chiefs as well as the principal chieftain of the entire Shawnee Nation. The Kishpoko sept produced the tribe's best warriors and its war chiefs. Like his father before him and his own children after him, Puckeshinwa belonged to the Kishpoko sept.

Puckeshinwa also belonged to the panther *unsoma*, or clan. All Shawnee, except for a few miserable outcasts, belonged to one of twelve unsomas. A child usually belonged to the unsoma of his or her father. Sometimes, however, the elders of the community interpreted omens in the natural world or traits displayed by the child as signs that the child belonged to his or her mother's unsoma, or perhaps to an unsoma of neither parent. Each unsoma had a particular animal as its totem, or symbol. The totem animal represented qualities that members of the unsoma were thought to share. Among the qualities associated with the panther unsoma were strength, speed, and daring.

Shawnee leaders meet with British officers to negotiate a truce after Pontiac's War. The speaker—possibly Puckeshinwa, Tecumseh's father—holds a belt. The Shawnee and other tribes declared war and sealed pacts by exchanging belts. *(Photo by C/Z HARRIS from Library of Congress collection)*

According to Shawnee tradition, Puckeshinwa was born some-where in the south. As a young man he lived in various parts of Pennsylvania. He had a reputation for skill with languages and acted as an interpreter during meetings among the Shawnee, the Delaware, and the whites. Some Shawnee accounts say that Puckeshinwa was one of the Native Americans who arranged the truce with the British after British forces captured Fort Duquesne in 1758. If so, he left the area soon afterward, for he spent the late 1750s in Alabama.

Although the tribes of Alabama had earlier resisted large-scale settlement by the Shawnee, a few Shawnee villages had taken root in Creek territory. To these villages came Puckenshinwa, by this time a mature man. There he met and married a girl named Methoataske. Her origins are unclear; some sources say that she was a Creek. One of the white civilians who was present at the 1810 meeting at Grouseland later claimed that he had chatted with Tecumseh about his parents. According to this man, Tecumseh had said that his mother was a Cherokee captive who had been adopted into the Shawnee tribe, the Pekowi sept, and the turtle unsoma. There is no evidence, however, that this conversation really occurred. After Tecumseh's death, some Native Americans who had known his family insisted that Methoataske was a full Shawnee, born of Shawnee parents. Again, there is no evidence to support this claim, which may have been an attempt to make Tecumseh a "pure" Shawnee hero. The details of Tecumseh's parentage, like many other facts about his life, are lost in the murk of anecdote and rumor.

Puckeshinwa spent a few years in Alabama and started a family there. He and Methoataske had a son named Chiksika and a daughter named Tecumpease. Then, sometime in the early 1760s, Puckeshinwa took his family north to the Shawnee settlements in the Ohio valley. Another son, Sauwauseekau, was born along the way. Some accounts say that Methoataske bore another daughter after arriving in Ohio. If so, the boy who was born in the spring of 1768 was the family's fifth child.

THE LEGEND OF TECUMSEH'S GRANDPARENTS

During the 19th century, several tall tales about Tecumseh worked their way into popular lore. In the mid-1820s Tecumseh's only surviving brother, Tenskwatawa, originally named Lalawethika, told a white chronicler an amazing story about his and his siblings' parentage.

Tenskwatawa declared that his grandfather had been a Creek warrior who lived in South Carolina. The governor of South Carolina at that time had a beautiful young daughter. One day this daughter saw a group of Indian men visiting her father. She was so impressed with their noble bearing that she decided then and there that she must have an Indian husband. The governor considered all the Indian men of the region and finally invited a handsome, courageous, and dignified Creek warrior to meet his daughter. The daughter fell in love with the warrior, and he with her. They were married, after which they lived among her people.

The happy couple had a son who took up Indian ways, living in the forest. He traveled from tribe to tribe and decided that he most admired the Shawnee. The Shawnee welcomed him and adopted him into their tribe. His name was Puckeshinwa. Thus Tecumseh and Tenskwatawa, the Shawnee Prophet, were the great-grandsons of a former governor of South Carolina.

Tenskwatawa's tale was both startling and romantic. Unfortunately, it was not true. He told it only after all the other members of his family were dead. In all the years before then, no one in or outside the family had ever suggested such a history. Nor was the relationship between the governor's daughter and the Creek warrior mentioned in any chronicles, letters, journals, or other records from South Carolina. And, as historian Bil Gilbert points out, "as sure as gossip is juicy," such a story would have been very well publicized indeed. The whole story was a fabrication, perhaps invented by Tenskwatawa for his own amusement at the expense of a gullible listener. There is no reason to believe that Tecumseh had any white blood. He was a Native American through and through.

Historians have been unable to determine exactly where Pucke-shinwa and his family lived at the time. There was a large Shawnee village called Chalahgawtha near the present-day site of Oldtown, Ohio. It is likely that Puckeshinwa had settled not far from that community, but the exact location of his home is unknown. Some historians have recorded Tecumseh's birthplace as a Shawnee village known as Piqua or Old Piqua, on the Mad River. In his book *God Gave Us This Country*, historian Bil Gilbert suggests that during the summer and fall Puckeshinwa's family lived in a village on Darby Creek, near its junction with the Scioto River. During the winter and early spring they lived with other families in a hunting camp on the Little Miami River, not far from the modern city of Xenia, Ohio. Tecumseh himself is said to have told people that he was born on the Little Miami and that he spent much of his boyhood there.

Methoataske, Tecumseh's mother, most likely followed Shawnee traditions concerning childbirth. When her time to give birth drew near, she left the main community. Accompanied by a woman friend or relative, she went to a prepared, secluded spot not far away. There, in a temporary shelter, she gave birth. She then remained in the birthing place with her newborn baby for several days so that both could rest and gain strength. Then she returned to the settlement and introduced the baby to family and community.

The special circumstances of Tecumseh's birth and naming have become a legend. The Shawnee claimed that as he was born, probably on the night of March 9, a giant meteor blazed a glittering trail of fire across the sky. To the Shawnee, meteors—or shooting stars—were part of the world of gods and spirits that surrounded human life. The meteor was a powerful, secretive panther spirit that sometimes crouched along forest trails waiting to punish evildoers and help good people. From time to time this lurking panther spirit leaped across the sky in a fiery blaze.

Such an omen was too powerful to be ignored. The infant was at once recognized as a member of his father's unsoma, the panther. Now it was time to give him a name. Shawnee names were

Tecumseh's birthplace in Ohio undoubtedly looked much like this typical Shawnee village. *(Cincinnati Historical Society, negative B-95-001)*

generally descriptive phrases that had something to do with the individual's unsoma totem; for example, a child who belonged to the turtle unsoma might be given a name that meant Lover of Water. Puckeshinwa's new son would have a name that referred to the panther spirit of the meteor.

The child was named Tecumseh, which was part of a phrase that meant "one who lies waiting to cross the path of living things." (This particular spelling of the leader's name became widely accepted, although according to some Shawnee speakers *Tecumthe* or *Tekamthi* would more closely resemble the way the name was pronounced.) Any Shawnee who heard the name would recognize that it referred to both the panther spirit *and* the meteor. For this reason Indians who later explained the meaning of Tecumseh's name to whites gave different translations, including Shooting Star, Crouching Panther, He Who Waits, and The Panther Crosses the Sky. The name Tecumseh encompasses all these meanings.

No details of Tecumseh's childhood are known. If, as an adult, Tecumseh spoke to whites about his early life, the conversations were not recorded. But it is reasonable to think that Tecumseh's boyhood was much like that of any typical young Shawnee of his day. Among the Shawnee, a child was to some extent raised by the whole community. Small children moved freely around their villages. The Shawnee used a whistling code in which each syllable of a child's name was represented by a particular note. At a very young age a boy or girl learned to recognize his or her whistled name and to respond to it from anywhere in the village. Grown men continued to use their name whistles to call to one another when they were hunting or on the war path.

Although each child lived with his or her family, all the adults in the village considered it their responsibility to watch, discipline, and teach all the children. Pride and shame were the tools that Shawnee adults used to discipline children. They publicly praised children for good behavior. A child who behaved badly was criticized and embarrassed in front of the rest of the community.

Shawnee men fished, hunted, and made war. Often they were away from home for long stretches of time. Women were the tribe's farmers and crafts workers. A woman carried her baby with her as she worked in the garden plots, gathered firewood, or carried water from the stream to her house. The baby was usually strapped to a device called a cradleboard, which the woman could hang from a convenient tree or carry on her back. Children who were old enough to walk roamed and played in the village, with the older children looking after the younger.

Play merged with education when girls began imitating the actions of their mothers and older sisters. They learned to plant, tend crops, sew, and cook by mimicking the older women. Cooking was a skill that was especially prized by the Shawnee. Their principal food was corn, which they ground into flour. Shawnee women were famous for the cornbreads and corn cakes they made from this flour. Members of other tribes and even some whites looked forward to visiting Shawnee villages because they knew that they would be offered delicious food. Families ate a morning meal together, and throughout the day the women and girls of each house kept stew cooking so that family members or friends could eat whenever they wanted. The Shawnee shared food communally, so that no one in the village went hungry as long as someone had food.

While girls began learning the arts of farming and housekeeping, boys were encouraged to play rambunctious games that nurtured their bravery and pride. Some of these pastimes were children's versions of favorite Shawnee sports such as ball games. Other games were mock warfare. At the age of five or six, boys received child-sized versions of Shawnee tools and weapons, such as bows and arrows and tomahawks. They learned how to use these items by watching the older men. Much of a Shawnee youth's education came from mimicking the accomplished hunters, warriors, and athletes.

In addition, young boys were expected to explore the forest beyond the village clearing. This activity served the useful function of driving away crows, deer, raccoons, and other creatures that might steal food from the women's fields. It also introduced the boys to the basics of woodcraft. As they played they learned to observe animals' habits, to read trails, and to move quietly through the dense growth. This early training helped prepare boys for a life of hunting, and it was vitally important.

A Shawnee man's standing in the community depended on his success as a hunter. A woman might decide to divorce a man who was unskilled or unlucky in the hunt because he was a bad provider. A man, on the other hand, could divorce a woman who was a bad farmer, homemaker, or mother. In fact, one story about Tecumseh illustrates this fact. Anthony Shane, the son of a French-Canadian father and a Shawnee mother, lived in Chalahgawtha and knew Tecumseh. In his recollections of Tecumseh he related that a beautiful young Shawnee woman lived with Tecumseh for several years around 1800. One day Tecumseh caught a large turkey to serve to guests. The woman did not prepare the turkey properly, at least according to Tecumseh's standards, and he ordered her to pack her things and leave his house.

Such domestic problems were probably the last thing on Tecumseh's mind during the early 1770s when he was a small child. Although he was the son of a respected war chieftain, he received no special privileges in the community. He was just another child in a village that lived by an age-old seasonal rhythm. Spring and early summer were for planting. Summer brought long days of fishing and hunting, as well as many festivals and rituals, including the Green Corn Dance of midsummer, held to honor the gods for their gift of food. Summer was also a time for traveling, visiting friends and relatives near and far. Fall brought the harvest, a time of great celebration when corn and other crops were gathered and prepared for the winter. In the fall the men

Like other young Shawnee men, Techumseh proved his skills on far-ranging hunting trips.   (*Photo by C/Z HARRIS from Library of Congress collection*)

went on long hunts, bringing back game that the women would preserve for the winter by smoking or drying it. The Shawnee spent the harsh Ohio valley winters wrapped in animal furs, telling tales around the fire during the long nights.

After the French and Indian War, life grew more unsettled every year for the Shawnee and the other tribes of the Ohio River valley. Frontier skirmishes were more frequent; Long Knives were more numerous. Tension between the whites and the Indians was rising fast.

In 1774 the tension erupted into violence. Although the Shawnee had repeatedly told British authorities that they would not permit surveyors to enter their hunting grounds in Kentucky, a group of surveyors did so that spring. The intruders represented a number of prominent Virginians, including George Washington and Patrick Henry, who were eager to claim land along the Ohio River. The Shawnee captured the surveyors, destroyed their equipment, and sent them home unharmed, warning them not to return. At the same time, a Cherokee war party attacked a party of Pennsylvania traders not far away. John Connolly, the leader of Pittsburgh's civilian defense force, or militia, blamed the Shawnee for both attacks and encouraged a band of white thugs to go out and kill some Shawnee.

Worse events were soon to follow. A group of Mingo were living in a village near what is now Steubenville, Ohio. Their leader was a chieftain named Logan, who was friendly toward the British. On April 30 some of the Mingo crossed the river to buy milk from a white settler who lived opposite their village. There they met a group of rowdy frontiersmen who got the Indians drunk, faked a shooting contest so that the Indian men would empty their guns, and then savagely slaughtered all thirteen Mingo. Among the dead were Logan's father, brother, and sister. The frontiersmen also killed several Shawnee who came to investigate the gunshots.

When the massacre was discovered, the Indians were appalled. Missionary John Hockewelder wrote, "It is indescribable, how enraged the relations of the murdered became, on seeing such abominable acts committed without cause, and even by some white men who had always pretended to be their friends." The Indians were not the only ones to be horrified. Many whites condemned the killings. Thomas Jefferson of Virginia called them "inhuman and indecent." The first reaction of most whites on the frontier, however, was fear. They were terrified that the Indians would seek revenge in a murderous rampage against them.

Their fears were unfounded. Logan declared that he did not want full-scale war but that he would kill one white for every Mingo who had died. He did so, and then the killing stopped. Rather, it would have stopped, except for Connolly of Pittsburgh, who eagerly turned the events into an excuse to promote war against the Shawnee. Connolly lied to Lord Dunmore, governor of Virginia, telling him that the Shawnee were taking the scalps of women and children. The goal of the Shawnee, said Connolly, was the extermination of all the whites in the Ohio valley.

The governor responded to this alarming news with prompt, decisive action, just as Connolly had hoped. He launched a campaign that has come to be known as Lord Dunmore's War. He claimed that his reason for going to war was to protect the frontier whites from possible Indian violence. There was another reason, however, and it was perhaps even more pressing. The British colonists, on the verge of declaring their independence from Britain, were increasingly restless with the British government's limits on their expansion westward. Dunmore was under great pressure from the people of Virginia—including men whom Americans have come to regard as their national heroes—to "settle" the Indian problem so that the Virginians could survey, sell, and occupy the Indians' land.

Because the Shawnee were considered the most warlike and troublesome tribe of the Ohio valley, Dunmore felt that his most effective strategy would be to attack them. He decided to wipe out the Shawnee villages along the Scioto River. If all went well, he would not only kill a large number of warriors in battle but, by destroying the tribe's homes and crops, force the survivors to leave the region.

Dunmore's plan of battle was simple. With 1,500 men, both regular troops and militia, from eastern Virginia he would go to Fort Pitt. Then he and his men would descend the Ohio River using traders' canoes and flatboats. They would meet another group of 1,500 troops and militiamen from western Virginia under the command of Colonel Andrew Lewis. Together these forces would attack the Shawnee communities across the Ohio.

The Shawnee were aware of Dunmore's plans and made preparations of their own. First they tried to find allies. The Chicksaw and the Creek turned them down, as did the tribes of the Iroquois Confederacy. Even the other tribes of the Ohio valley refused to get involved. The chieftains of these tribes felt that, as Dunmore was attacking only the Shawnee, he was the Shawnee's problem. Only the Mingo, the Delaware, and the Wyandot contributed a few fighters, warriors who did not agree with their chieftains. In the end the Shawnee mustered only about 700 fighters. They were led by a war chieftain named Cornstalk, a well-respected commander in chief. One of the lesser commanders was Puckeshinwa, Tecumseh's father. The other chief lieutenants were war chieftains Black Hoof, Black Fish, and Blue Jacket—the former white captive. Chiksika, Tecumseh's fourteen-year-old brother, was a member of the war party, which included every able-bodied man from the Shawnee villages.

By the time Cornstalk had gathered his warriors, Lewis's party was camped on a hill called Point Pleasant, waiting for Dunmore. Cornstalk massed his men across the Ohio from Point Pleasant and formed a typical Shawnee plan—that is, a plan that was bold and aggressive. Instead of waiting for the two groups of Virginians to meet, cross the river, and attack, he would strike quickly and try to knock out Lewis's group. He led more than half of his warriors six miles upstream. There the men cut trees and built rafts. On the night of October 9, 1774, they floated and swam across the river and advanced silently on Point Pleasant.

Just before dawn, two frontiersmen from Lewis's party were out hunting turkeys when they sighted the approaching Shawnee war party. By rushing back to camp and sounding the alarm, these two hunters prevented Cornstalk's attack from being a complete surprise. Lewis's men had time to pull themselves together and mount a sound defense of the hill.

The fighting went on all day, until the ground under the trees was red with blood, eerily echoing the color of the brilliant fall foliage above. Finally the Shawnee ran out of ammunition and withdrew across the river. They had failed to drive the British from their hilltop stronghold, so the British claimed a victory. On the other hand, the Shawnee had only about 50 casualties, whereas the British counted 81 dead and 140 wounded. Having killed more of the enemy than they had lost, the Shawnee also claimed victory. In reality the battle of Point Pleasant was a bloody stalemate.

One of the Shawnee casualties was Puckeshinwa. As the Shawnee prepared to retreat to the river, he was hit in the chest by a musket ball. Chiksika was at his side. The dying Puckeshinwa asked Chiksika to swear that he would never make peace with the Virginians. Chiksika made that vow. Puckeshinwa then told Chiksika to take good care of his younger brothers and to see that they received a warrior's training, and this too Chiksika promised to do. Puckeshinwa died and was buried in a hastily dug, hidden grave in the forest. Then the Shawnee hurried across the river.

Cornstalk regrouped his men and called a council at Chalahgawtha. By this time the Shawnee knew that Lewis and his surviving men had crossed the river and were marching toward them, while Dunmore and his militiamen advanced from a different direction. Friendly white traders who were present at the Shawnee council later reported that Cornstalk faced the assembled chieftains and said, "The Long Knives are upon us by two routes. Shall we turn and fight them? Shall we kill our squaws and children and then fight until we are killed ourselves?" No one answered. Cornstalk then drove his tomahawk into a post in the center of the council site and declared, "Since you are not inclined to fight, I will go and make peace."

Cornstalk met with Dunmore to discuss the terms of peace. Both men knew that the British position was now stronger than that of the Shawnee and that the militiamen wanted nothing better than to cut a violent swath through Shawnee country. To save their villages, the Shawnee signed a treaty that gave up their claim to hunting grounds in Kentucky. They also agreed to turn all captives over to the British and to allow the British to travel freely on the Ohio River. In return, Dunmore promised that the British would neither hunt nor settle north of the Ohio.

The aftermath of Lord Dunmore's War was a sudden increase in white activity in Kentucky. By the mid-1770s there were about 10,000 whites living there. In addition, the British had increased their military presence at Fort Pitt and built a fort called Fort Randolph at Point Pleasant. To distance themselves from the army and the Long Knives, the Shawnee migrated into the western part of their territory. By 1777 their principal settlements were along the Big Miami and Little Miami rivers.

By this time, the British colonies in North America had declared themselves independent. The former colonists were at war with Britain. Once again the Native Americans of eastern North America found themselves squeezed between two warring foreign powers. This time the rivals were the British and the Americans. The British had forced the Indians to agree to unfair and humiliating treaties. At the same time, they were longtime trading partners whose goods the Indians had come to value. The Americans, on the other hand, were all too eager to overrun the western lands. The Long Knives and the frontier settlers, with their disregard for both British law and Indian tradition, had shown the Native Americans what they could expect if the Americans succeeded in winning their independence. In general, the Indians were more likely to side with the British than with the Americans.

Cornstalk tried to keep the Shawnee neutral. His policy was to appear sympathetic to both sides and to make promises to neither. However, a number of the young warriors, including Chiksika, were more than willing to attack American settlers in Kentucky. Encouraged and sometimes armed by the British, their raiding parties began killing settlers. In 1777 Black Fish, the Shawnee war chieftain who had been one of Cornstalk's lieutenants at Point Pleasant, led several attacks on Boonesborough, a Kentucky settlement founded by Daniel Boone, who was to become one of the most famous of the American frontiersmen.

In October of 1777, Cornstalk went to speak with Captain Matthew Arbuckle at Fort Randolph, which was now an American outpost. There are various accounts of why Cornstalk visited Arbuckle: Some sources say that he intended to warn Arbuckle that he could no longer control the hot-blooded young warriors of his tribe, while others say that he was simply helping some American mapmakers who were at the fort. Either way, the visit was an unlucky one. While Cornstalk was at Fort Randolph, Indians killed an American settler nearby. A mob of angry frontiersmen stormed the fort and killed Cornstalk and four accompanying Shawnee.

News of this cowardly and unfair murder convinced many Indians that they could no longer remain neutral and made the ones who had wanted to fight even more determined to drive out the whites or kill them. Shawnee and Mingo war parties stepped up their assaults on the frontier settlements. In January 1778 Daniel Boone was leading a party of settlers from Boonesborough on an expedition into the forests to collect salt from certain river ponds. Unable to hunt every day because of the presence of Indian war parties throughout the woods, the settlers desperately needed the salt to preserve their meat.

The salt gatherers were taken prisoner by a party of 100 Delaware and Shawnee warriors led by Black Fish. The Indians took the sixteen men back to their villages and adopted them into the tribe. Black Fish himself adopted Boone. The events of the following months are a topic of controversy among frontier historians. Did Boone pretend to be satisfied with his new life simply to gain increasing freedom so that he could ultimately escape, or did he collaborate with the Indians to ensure his own safety? All that is known for certain is that he attended several war councils, including a meeting with British officers and a session at which Indian chieftains planned another attack on Boonesborough. After four months as a Shawnee, he escaped while hunting and fled to Boonesborough, leaving the other adopted men behind. He warned the settlers to expect an Indian attack. A few months later the Indians did attack Boonesborough but failed to take the well-fortified settlement. Within days a force of mounted militiamen had crossed the Ohio River and attacked Shawnee settlements in retaliation for the assault on Boonesborough. Black Fish died of a wound he received in one of these attacks.

As for Boone, some suspicion lingered that he had had dishonorable dealings with the Indians, the British, or both. However, a court-martial cleared him of all charges, and most people eventually concluded that he had acted to save his life and in the settlers' best interests.

It is likely that Tecumseh saw Boone during the frontiersman's sojourn with the Shawnee given that Black Fish, who adopted Boone, maintained a close connection with the children of Puckeshinwa. Tecumseh and his family had had to make many adjustments after Puckeshinwa's death. Tecumseh was six years old when Chiksika came home alone from Point Pleasant bearing the sad news that Puckeshinwa had been killed. Chiksika tried to provide for his mother, brothers, and sisters, but he was hard-pressed to provide food for a family that was rather large by Shawnee standards. It soon became even larger. Methoataske had been pregnant when Puckeshinwa left for battle, and after his death she gave birth to triplets, all boys. One of the babies soon died, but two lived. Their names were Lalawethika and Kumskaukau.

As was the Shawnee custom, Puckeshinwa's friends and relatives stepped in to help take care of the family. They provided fish and game. One of the most helpful was Black Fish, who took on the role of guardian to Tecumseh and the other young children—until he was killed in May of 1779. When Tecumpease, Tecumseh's older sister, married a warrior named Wasabogoa, he too contributed to the family's welfare.

The year 1779 brought still more changes to Tecumseh's family. Cornstalk's death and the militia raids into Ohio had frightened and discouraged some Shawnee. In addition, a sizable portion of the tribe still wished to remain neutral in the Revolutionary War. The result was a splitting of the tribe. In the summer of 1779, about 1,000 Shawnee, perhaps a third of the tribe, left the Ohio River valley. They migrated west through Indiana and Illinois and then south along the Mississippi River to south-eastern Missouri, where they eventually settled. Among those who left was Methoataske, Tecumseh's mother. It is said that she was accompanied by her second daughter, born between Sau-wauseekau and Tecumseh. The other children remained in Ohio.

Such family separations were not unheard-of among the Shawnee and some other Native American tribes. Parents some-times sent their children to live with and be raised by relatives. In any case, it was the duty of the father's kinfolk, not the mother's, to take care of children. Whatever her reasons, Methoataske de-parted, and no one considered her departure to be strange or unnatural. Most likely other Shawnee families were also broken in this great splitting of the tribe. By the middle of 1779 Tecumseh had lost his father, his mother, his guardian Black Fish. Yet he retained considerable prestige as the son of an honored war chieftain. He had a protector and guide in his brother Chiksika and a beloved friend in his sister Tecumpease, who took him into her home. Above all, Tecumseh had a clear path to follow and a place to secure among his people. He would be what Puckeshinwa had wanted him to be. At eleven years of age, Tecumseh was on the verge of becoming a warrior.

NOTES

p. 33   "as sure as gossip is juicy." Gilbert, p. 53.

pp. 39–40 "It is indescribable . . ." Quoted in Sanford Wexler, *Westward Expansion: An Eyewitness History* (New York: Facts On File, 1991), p. 24.

p. 40   "inhuman and indecent." Quoted in Robert Cwiklik, *Tecumseh* (New York: Chelsea House, 1993), p. 28.

p. 42   "The Long Knives are upon us . . ." Quoted in Bil Gilbert, *God Gave Us This Country* (New York: Atheneum, 1989), p. 69.

THE YOUNG
WARRIOR

Several white boys lived among the Shawnee while Tecumseh was growing up. Anthony Shane, the son of a trader and a Shawnee woman, was one. Three others were the sons of Kentucky settlers and had been captured and adopted. One of them, Stephen Ruddell, became friendly with Tecumseh, who called Ruddell Big Fish. Some years later Ruddell returned to white society with his Shawnee wife. He became a minister and wrote an account of his Shawnee childhood; in his writings he revealed great admiration for the young Tecumseh.

Ruddell claimed that Tecumseh was a natural leader among the boys of his age and that he always had a set of loyal followers whom he directed in mock battles and other activities. Tecumseh, said Ruddell, was always the best at everything: sports, hunting, using the bow and arrow or war club. He was also the bravest and most honorable of all the boys. Ruddell wrote his account after Tecumseh had become famous, and some historians feel that he probably exaggerated to glorify Tecumseh—and perhaps to elevate himself as one of Tecumseh's friends in his youth. Yet Shane's recollections, together with remarks that various Shawnee made over the years to traders and other white friends, affirm that Tecumseh was indeed a strong, agile, skillful youth whose leadership qualities were recognized by those around him.

Becoming a Shawnee warrior was not easy. Many of the training exercises that a young man had to perform were intended to build character as well as skill. Boys were taught to endure discomfort, hardship, and even pain without complaining or showing fear. They were expected to be fearless and honest at all times. One typical exercise took place during the winter and required a boy to break a hole in the ice of the nearest river or lake and plunge into the frigid water—every day for the entire season. Another exercise took place when a boy was ten or twelve years old. The elder warriors smeared the boy's face with charcoal and sent him off armed but alone, telling him not to return until he could bring back some kind of game to offer as food to the community. The black smears on the boy's face were a sign to everyone he met that he was undertaking a quest and should not be aided.

Boys who gave up during these trials because of fear or exhaustion, or who lied, or who blamed others for their own shortcomings, were regarded as having acted in a most unwarriorlike manner. Such behavior was one of the very few offenses for which a Shawnee youth could receive physical punishment. The elders would beat or whip a cowardly or dishonest boy, often rather severely. If the boy endured the punishment without whining or crying, he was thought to have regained some of his lost honor.

After he had demonstrated success in his first solo hunt, a young Shawnee man was allowed to join the hunting parties that regularly went out from each Shawnee village on expeditions of a few days or a few weeks. Certainly Tecumseh would have done so. And in the troubled world of the Ohio valley in the late 18th century, hunting parties could easily become war parties.

Tecumseh's first experience of war was one of the raids on the Shawnee villages in the late 1770s. He may even have been living with Black Fish when Black Fish was attacked and wounded. Whether the ten- or eleven-year-old Tecumseh took part in the fighting on these occasions is unknown. If not, he soon had other opportunities.

The new Continental Army was busy fighting the British in the east. George Washington and the other military and government leaders of the former colonies could not spare troops to fight Indians on the frontier. They informed the frontiersmen that they would have to look after themselves for the time being.

Some of the frontiersmen were ready, willing, and able to take up the challenge.

One of the most active and capable militia leaders in Kentucky was George Rogers Clark. Beginning in 1780 he led several raids into Ohio, where he burned Shawnee villages to the ground. Casualties were not high, for each time most of the Shawnee were able to retreat into the forest. The Shawnee responded with a series of bloody raids far into Kentucky. From the Ohio River to what is now Tennessee, no isolated homestead was safe. People had to crowd into the few fortified settlements to survive. The raids by both sides back and forth across the river became too numerous to count. The Indian war parties and the militiamen fought repeatedly in the same places.

The Shawnee also attacked and harrassed American boats on the Ohio River. Often they were accompanied and aided by British officials called Indian agents. The British hoped that by supporting the Indians against the settlers they could keep the Ohio valley under British influence, even if the coastal colonies succeeded in their bid for independence.

Around this time, according to many histories, Tecumseh took part in his first battle as a warrior. Details are hazy, but he may have been less than fourteen years old at the time. Legend says that Chiksika allowed Tecumseh to join a war party for the first time. The Shawnee engaged in a skirmish with a band of Kentuckians—some sources say it happened in Kentucky, while others say it happened in Ohio. The two forces exchanged gunfire, and Chiksika was hit, although the wound was not serious. The story goes that Tecumseh, surrounded by militiamen and overwhelmed with nervousness and fear, deserted the battle and hid in the forest. Later he rejoined the war party, deeply humiliated, and swore that never again would he do such a thing.

The Long Knives of Kentucky called 1782 the Year of Blood. It was a year of exceptional violence on the frontier, and much blood was shed on both sides. Clark attacked the Shawnee villages again. A group of warriors from several tribes, led by British Indian agents, attacked a Kentucky fort and ambushed its defenders. Yet even in this bloody year several incidents stood out as especially horrible.

The first occurred at Gnaddenhutten, a village on the Tuscarawas River in eastern Ohio. Gnaddenhutten had been founded by missionaries and was the home of a group of peaceful Delaware who had converted to Christianity. Frontiersman David Williamson claimed that the Gnaddenhutten Delaware were being directed by the British to act against the Americans, although not a single piece of evidence supported this claim. Williamson assembled a bloodthirsty militia band and attacked Gnaddenhutten. Striking while the Indians were at prayer, the militia rounded up twenty unarmed, defenseless men and about seventy women and children, tied their hands, and systematically killed them. One of the militiamen, Charles Builderback, was a barrel-maker and had brought with him one of his tools, a heavy wooden mallet. He crushed the skulls of thirteen Delaware and then handed the mallet to a friend, saying, "My arm fails me. Go on in the same way. I think I have done pretty well."

Some whites shared the Indians' horror at these killings. Yet to the Indians, Gnaddenhutten was proof that the whites thought that Indians were not fit to live. In later years, Tecumseh would point to Gnaddenhutten when telling Native Americans of many tribes that they faced an enemy who was determined to wipe them off the face of the earth.

The massacre at Gnaddenhutten lit the fires of revenge in every Indian village in the Ohio valley. A few weeks after the massacre, a war party of 1,000 Delaware and Wyandot attacked a column of militiamen, killing 100 or so and capturing 11. Although they had failed to capture Williamson, who had turned and fled before the fighting began, the Indians executed their captives. They subjected William Crawford, a friend of George Washington and the leader of the militia column, to hours of dreadful torture before he died. One captive escaped to spread the word of Crawford's ghastly end.

To the Indians Crawford's death was fair payment for the atrocity of Gnaddenhutten. After all, they argued, not only had Crawford failed to punish Williamson, but he had been marching with Williamson to attack the Indians again. Whites across North America, however, saw matters differently. Crawford had not even been at Gnaddenhutten. His torture, even more than his death, was evidence of a savage brutality that could not be allowed to continue. In the end, the Gnaddenhutten massacre and the torture of Crawford simply hardened the hearts of the opposing sides.

David Williamson managed to escape the Indians' wrath, but Charles Builderback was not so lucky. Seven years later a Shawnee war party captured him and recognized him as "the butcher of Gnaddenhutten." The Shawnee tortured Builderback for hours before smashing his skull with their hatchets. As one historian of the frontier wars has written, "During the Indian wars few men of either race died more horribly than Builderback."

Torture had become part of frontier warfare and was practiced by both sides. Yet in 1783 Tecumseh, still a junior warrior, took a stand against it. According to Stephen Ruddell, Tecumseh was part of a war party that captured a flatboat on the Ohio. All but one of the boat's crewmen were killed in the fighting. The Shawnee took the survivor captive and then burned him at the stake. Tecumseh did nothing to interfere, but the sight filled him with loathing and disgust. According to one version of the story, Tecumseh stood in front of the war party and delivered a long, passionate speech about the cowardice of torturing a helpless prisoner. It is, however, unlikely that a youth would have harangued and criticized a body of seasoned warriors in this way. More probably Tecumseh expressed his views later, perhaps privately to Ruddell. At any rate, Ruddell said that Tecumseh vowed never again to allow such a thing to happen if he could prevent it. Events many years later would show that Tecumseh lived up to that vow.

If 1782 was the Year of Blood, 1783 was the Year of Peace—at least on one front. The Treaty of Paris brought the American Revolution to an end. The victorious Americans, independent of Britain, could now turn their attention to taming their western frontier.

The British, still hoping to keep the Americans from getting a firm grip on the lands west of the original colonies, remained very much involved in the turmoil of the frontier. British troops refused to withdraw from several forts around the Great Lakes, and British Indian agents continued to support the tribes in their attacks on settlers.

Meanwhile, the new American government had plans for Ohio. In desperate need of cash, the government wanted to sell part of Ohio to settlers and to the real-estate investors called land speculators. The rest of Ohio would be awarded to soldiers who had served in the Revolution. First, of course, the government had to obtain some sort of claim to Ohio from the Indians. It did so at a series of very shady treaty conferences. Explains historian R. David Edmunds:

> In several instances the Indians who attended the conferences had absolutely no legitimate claims to the lands in question, and more often the warriors who made their

A somewhat romanticized view of Tecumseh saving the lives of prisoners taken by the Shawnee. Whatever the truth of this incident, Tecumseh certainly regarded the torture of helpless captives as cowardly. *(Library of Congress)*

marks on the documents were, at best, minor chiefs who
did not represent the wishes of their people. Although
the government claimed that the treaties were valid,
most Shawnees regarded them as a travesty and had no
intention of abiding by them.

The Shawnee were furious when surveyors and settlers moved
north of the Ohio River and began clearing the forest. The Shawnee
chieftain Kehenepelity declared to a government official in 1786,
"As to the lands, God gave us this country! We do not understand
measuring out the lands. It is all ours! You say you have goods for
our women and children. You may keep your goods and give them
to other nations. We will have none of them."

Although the majority of the Indians north of the Ohio River
insisted that the land was still theirs, in 1787 Congress passed the
Northwest Ordinance. This law was designed to extend American government into the lands north and west of the Ohio River.
It established the Northwest Territory and stated that the territory would eventually be made into three to five new states. It
was clear that the United States had no intention of honoring the
Indians' claim.

Soon the Shawnee were at war again. Tecumseh joined a war
party led by his brother Chiksika. They spent months on the road,
traveling through the region south of the Ohio River, fighting
side by side with men of many tribes. In 1788 they were in
east-central Tennessee preparing to help a Cherokee band attack
an American stockade. According to accounts written in the 19th
century, Chiksika had a vision of his own death in the coming
battle. He told his comrades and his brother about it but declared
that he was not afraid. He wanted to die in battle like his father.
Sure enough, Chiksika was fatally wounded during the attack on
the stockade.

This would not be the only time that Tecumseh and important
people in his life would be touched by a prophecy or vision of
coming death. Tales of such occurrences were common among
some Native American peoples and were widely repeated. Generally they were written down years later, by people who heard the

story at second, third, or even fourth hand. At this point in time there is no way to determine whether Chiksika really prophesied his own death. But the story impressed people, both Shawnee and white, and it became part of the informal history of the frontier.

Tecumseh and a few other members of the war party remained in the south for a few years after Chiksika's death. Little is known about this period in Tecumseh's life, except that he assumed the leadership of the small band of roving fighters. They stayed with many different friendly Indian communities, and they allied themselves with Creek and Cherokee warriors to fight the Long Knives in Alabama and perhaps as far south as Florida. Once Chiksika's follower, Tecumseh had become a war leader in his own right. These years not only gave him experience in commanding men and planning strategy but also introduced him to the cultures, villages, and chieftains of many Native American groups across the south. Later, when Tecumseh tried to form a union of all Indians, he would return to the south to preach his cause in these same villages.

While Tecumseh and his men were riding and fighting south of the Ohio River, a major military campaign was shaping up on the north bank of the river. The rush of white settlers into Ohio had caused the Shawnee to move their villages westward and northward yet again. Now they were based along the Maumee River in northwestern Ohio, near a number of Miami, Wyandot, and Ottawa settlements.

Leaders of these tribes and of the Delaware, Potawatomi, Kickapoo, and Chippewa tribes met—sometimes with the assistance of British Indian agents—to try to form an alliance. They could not agree on the best response to the white threat. Some tribes were willing to give up southern Ohio. Others wanted to keep southern Ohio but were reluctant to enter into all-out war. The most militant tribes were the Shawnee, led by Blue Jacket, and the Miami, led by Little Turtle. Their position was clear: Everything north of the Ohio must remain Indian land, and they were ready to fight. Although the attempt to form a loose alliance or confederation of tribes did not succeed, men from several tribes did fight side by side in the next round of battles. In fact, they fought so well that William Henry Harrison, who was present at one of those battles, called them "the finest light troops in the world."

The Americans had hoped that the Indians would accept the new treaties peacefully. When that did not happen, they prepared for war. President George Washington and Congress had created the first American federal army—about 1,200 officers and men—and sent part of it to the western frontier. The president now instructed Arthur St. Clair, the governor of the Northwest Territory, to raise another 1,500 militia troops from among the settlers in Kentucky and Ohio.

The commander of the American troops on the frontier was General Josiah Harmar of Philadelphia, an "undistinguished veteran of the American Revolution" who had "a fondness for the bottle." He and St. Clair led the American army into what military historian James M. Perry has called "one of the most disastrous, and unnecessary, campaigns in its history."

The campaign would undoubtedly have been more successful if it had been led by officers who had some experience in frontier and guerrilla fighting. Fat, conceited, and "no military genius," Harmar was an extremely poor choice for a frontier general. His force consisted of 700 regular troops and 1,500 militiamen, all ill-equipped and undisciplined—not the small, highly trained strike force needed for successful frontier combat. The militiamen were especially unpromising; many of them were unable to clean their guns because they did not know how to take them apart. Writes Perry:

> These were no ordinary militiamen; the troops being sent to Harmar were simply awful. Major Denny, a Revolutionary War veteran from western Pennsylvania . . . called the Kentuckians "misfits and loiterers" who were "raw and unused to the gun or the woods; indeed, many are without guns." The Pennsylvania militia was, if anything, even worse. Harmar said they were "hardly able to bear arms—such as old, infirm men and young boys."

"No one has a more contemptible opinion of the militia than I," said General Josiah Harmar, who reluctantly led a band of militiamen against the Ohio Indians. His men amply fulfilled his gloomy forebodings. *(Indiana Historical Society, negative A103)*

Harmar built a two-story stockade on the Ohio River and named it Fort Harmar. He enjoyed a comfortable life there, drinking wine and writing to his friends in Philadelphia about the abundant food of the region: "Venison, two or three inches deep in fat" and "cat fish of one hundreds pounds' weight." As for military training, Harmar tried to teach the basics of warfare from an old-fashioned military manual that he carried everywhere with him. Geared to traditional European-style warfare, with armies maneuvering on open battlefields, this manual would prove woefully ill-suited to the frontier forests.

Harmar and St. Clair built a post called Fort Washington, at the present-day site of Cincinnati, to serve as a launching point for the strike into the interior of Ohio. Harmar's two-pronged attack began in September 1790. Major John Hamtramck led a group of militiamen and about 100 regular troops up the Wabash River with orders to attack every Indian village they found. These attacks were supposed to keep the Indians busy so that Harmar could march his column up the Miami River to the Maumee, where he would attack the main Miami and Shawnee settlements.

Harmar's plan did not work very well for two reasons. First, Secretary of War Henry Knox had ordered Governor St. Clair to notify Patrick Murray, the British commander at Detroit, of the coming attack. Knox wanted to reassure Murray that the American army was not planning to attack the British-held fort. St. Clair sent this message, adding a request that Murray keep the information secret. Murray, of course, promptly relayed the information to the Indians. Some accounts say that he offered the Indians bounties for every American scalp or prisoner they brought to Detroit.

The Indians would probably have known what was happening even without Murray's help. They maintained their own network of spies, scouts, and informants. Well aware of Hamtramck's purpose, they simply slipped away from their villages when his column approached. Hamtramck and his men returned to Fort Washington after three weeks. They had burned a number of villages but had not fired a single shot.

Harmar's second prong was even less successful. He marched out of Fort Washington with 1,133 militiamen and 320 regulars. His officers, some of whom hated each other, were quarreling openly among themselves over who outranked whom. The disorganized force marched in two groups, with regimental flags waving and fifes and drums playing. The men averaged ten miles a day. Each night the Indians stealthily stole pack horses. The army lost so many pack horses that one officer suspected the horse drivers of a plot to demand damage money from the government.

In October Harmar arrived at Kekionga, the major Miami settlement, located where Fort Wayne, Indiana, now stands. Harmar found the Miami villages deserted and burned to the ground. He was "convinced that he had won a great victory without firing a shot"; in reality, Little Turtle had sacrificed his villages and hidden his people in the forest. The next day Harmar sent some scouts out under the command of Colonel John Hardin. Some of the men deserted and returned to the main force. When Hardin and the remainder of his men spotted Indian artifacts lying in a field, they split up and scrambled to collect plunder and souvenirs.

Now Little Turtle and Blue Jacket sprang the trap they had planned with the help of Simon Girty, a frontiersman and trader who fought on both sides during the war but generally allied himself with the Indians. When a band of Indians leaped out of ambush and opened fire, Hardin and his militia dropped their weapons and fled. The regulars stood their ground and were shot down.

The surviving militiamen ran back down the trail screaming, "For God's sake retreat! You will all be killed. There are Indians enough to eat you up!" They reached Harmar's camp. In his anger Harmar burned several deserted villages that his men had found and destroyed 20,000 bushels of corn that the Indians had buried. Then Harmar began to retreat. Hardin volunteered to lead a detachment back to Kekionga to ambush the Miami when they came home, and Harmar agreed. Some of Hardin's men were said to have burst into tears when they learned that they might have to fight again.

Little Turtle attacked Hardin's force as it crossed the Maumee River. One witness later said that the river was so full of American bodies that he could have crossed it without wetting his feet. Although he lost 120 men, Hardin reached Harmar's camp, where he claimed to have won a victory. "Others knew better; it had been a terrible defeat," says military historian James M. Perry. "The victory belonged to a great military commander, Little Turtle." Harmar's bedraggled and dispirited column hastened back to Fort Washington.

Many people criticized Harmar for not taking part in battle. George Washington said, "I expected little from the moment I heard he was a drunkard." Yet Washington must also bear some of the blame. He had given the command to the incompetent Harmar in the first place. His next mistake was worse: Washington turned the frontier military command over to Governor St. Clair, who insisted that he could lead a successful campaign against the Miami and Shawnee. According to Perry, "Harmar was a calamity; St. Clair would be a catastrophe."

Tecumseh and his warrior band returned to Ohio in early November 1790. They shared the rejoicing of the Shawnee and Miami, who were rebuilding their communities. Harmar's disastrous and ineffective campaign had made the Indians confident that they could defend themselves against further attacks. Fresh from his battle experience in the south, Tecumseh was accepted into the tribal councils as one of the war chiefs.

Throughout 1791 St. Clair prepared for his campaign. A native of Scotland who had fought as a British officer during the French and Indian War, St. Clair had switched sides during the American Revolution. He had commanded American troops against the British and for a short time had served as president of the Continental Congress. None of this, however, had equipped him to fight Indians.

President Washington summoned St. Clair to Philadelphia and tried to impress upon him a few truths about frontier fighting. The president concluded his remarks by saying, "General St. Clair, in three words, beware of surprise. Trust not the Indian; leave not your arms for the moment; and when you halt

A FRONTIER RENEGADE

The three Girty brothers were captured on the frontier as boys and spent eight years living in Indian villages: Simon with the Seneca, James with the Shawnee, and George with the Delaware. As adults the Girtys remained in a kind of half-world on the frontier, living sometimes among whites and sometimes among Indians. All of them spoke several Indian languages and were frequently in demand as interpreters.

Simon Girty became notorious in the Old Northwest as a renegade who fought on the side of Indians against whites. In reality, however, Girty's first loyalty was to himself. Although he cast his lot with the Indians, he was an agent in the pay of the British, who rewarded him with money and with land in Canada. And from time to time, when it suited his interests, Girty fought against the Indians.

Most of the time, though, Girty encouraged the Indians to attack Americans, and he took part in some of their raids. He boasted that while attacking an Ohio river flat-boat in 1779 he had killed Major David Rogers. In that same attack, however, the Indians captured another officer, Colonel John Campbell. Girty recognized Campbell as a former friend and neighbor from Pennsylvania and saved him

for the night be sure to fortify your camp. Again and again, General, beware of surprise!"

Like Harmar, St. Clair was a fat man who enjoyed eating, drinking, and comfortable living. He also suffered from gout, a painful disease that at times made it impossible for him to walk. He reached Fort Washington in May 1791 and found there a motley bunch of troops: drunkards, convicts, and layabouts. Their guns were in terrible shape, and many of them had no shoes. One of St. Clair's junior officers wrote that the troops were "generally wanting the essential stamina of soldiers. Picked up and recruited from the offscourings of large towns and cities; enervated by idleness, debaucheries, and every species of vice, it was impossible they could have been made competent to the arduous duties from torture and death. Several other times Girty intervened with his Indian friends to save the lives of whites whom he knew and liked. He even tried to save William Crawford, whom the Indians captured in revenge for the Gnaddenhutten massacre. This time, however, Girty failed to influence the Indians.

When Blue Jacket's forces were preparing for war with St. Clair and his army, Girty was one of Blue Jacket's spies. On the eve of battle, writes military historian James Perry, "Girty brought the warriors to their feet with a dramatic demonstration. He pulled a white egg from his pocket, saying, 'This represents the whites coming towards me, while my fingers encircling it represent our brotherhood of Indians here. What will be the outcome when they meet? See!' Then he crushed the shell and watched as the egg dripped on the ground. Girty said later that he had never seen Indians 'in greater heart to meet their enemy.'"

Years later, when the United States and Great Britain went to war, Girty—by then old and nearly blind—took refuge on his farm in Canada. An invading U.S. army wanted to burn his house down but was prevented from doing so by frontiersman Simon Kenton, whom Girty had twice saved from the Indians.

of Indian warfare." He also noted that the men were cowardly and that many of them deserted. Some of them joined the Indians, "the very foe we were to combat. . . . They were moreover, badly clothed, badly paid, and badly fed." The army signed a contract for military supplies with William Duer, a friend of Knox and Washington, who cheated St. Clair by providing leaky tents, ill-made shoes that wore out in a week, and other shoddy gear.

Despite these dismal omens, Major Denny, who had served under Harmar, was part of St. Clair's force. Harmar had told him, not very encouragingly, "You must go on the campaign—some will escape, and you may be among the number."

Throughout the summer, St. Clair tried to equip his ragged army and prepare it to march and to fight. During this time,

Tecumseh was not far away. Some accounts of his life even claim that several times he entered Fort Washington as a spy, looking and listening and learning what the army was planning. Whether or not he ever really spied on the Americans from inside the fort, he almost certainly did so from outside. A nearby hill offered a vantage point into the fort. From there Tecumseh and other scouts were able to keep an eye on the army's activities, which they reported to Little Turtle and Blue Jacket.

By September the army was as ready as it was ever going to be. St. Clair had to take action, for soon it would be winter. The doors of Fort Washington swung open and St. Clair's column—accompanied by about 60 women who were companions of some of the officers and men—began moving slowly and clumsily north through the forest. Progress was slow, partly because they lacked sufficient axes to clear a path and partly because St. Clair had to be carried in a litter much of the time; he was in too much pain to ride a horse.

In late October St. Clair ordered his men to build a stockade called Fort Jefferson on the present-day site of Greenville, Ohio. The stockade offered only a brief stop on a long and difficult

Fort Washington, where American forces prepared for an all-out attack on the Indians. Legend says that Tecumseh spied on their preparations from a nearby hilltop. *(Photo by C/Z HARRIS from Library of Congress collection)*

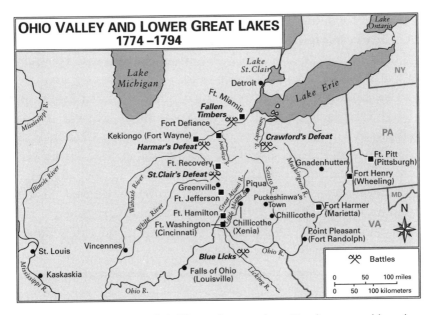

In the late 18th century, the Ohio River valley was the setting for many raids and skirmishes between whites and Indians and also for one of the most disastrous campaigns in American military history.

march. The weather turned cold. Food ran low. Desertions became more frequent even though St. Clair hanged several men for trying to desert. And when the column finally advanced on Kekionga, there were ominous signs that the Indians were watching. A soldier was scalped not far from camp one night. Finally St. Clair had to send some of the 300 regular troops back along his trail to keep the supply column in the rear from being looted by deserting militiamen. He had started out from Fort Washington with about 2,300 men, and now 1,500 remained. His assistant wrote, "Our prospects are gloomy. But the general is compelled to move on, as the only chance of continuing our little army."

When St. Clair made camp on an early November night, he had apparently forgotten Washington's words of warning. He erected no barricade and posted no guards. Indians began circling the camp after dark. Little Turtle launched his attack just before dawn. One white survivor wrote that "the firing of the enemy was preceded for about five minutes by the Indian yell, the first I had ever heard. Not terrible, as has been represented, but more resembling an infinitude of horse's bells suddenly opening to you than any other sound I could compare it to."

The battle lasted only three hours. Indians overran the camp, slaughtering soldiers and women. Some of the regular troops fought well, but the militia once again revealed their lack of experience and leadership. They ran like sheep. St. Clair's assistant called their conduct "cowardly to the most shameful degree." St. Clair, however, certainly did not distinguish himself. Rising from his bed of pain, he found that he was able to mount a horse after all. When the retreat began he took the lead, pounding down the trail as fast as his horse could go.

Instead of teaching the "savages" a lesson, Major General Arthur St. Clair suffered one of the most humiliating defeats in American military history. *(Photo by C/Z HARRIS from* The St. Clair Papers, *Cincinnati, 1882)*

The fleeing troops did not halt at Fort Jefferson but drove themselves on to Fort Washington. The return trip was accomplished much more speedily than the outward journey. St. Clair's defeat was even more bitter than Harmar's. Writes historian Perry:

> When the Americans began counting their dead, wounded, and missing, they discovered, to their horror, that they had lost more than half their army. It remains the worst defeat Indians ever inflicted on an American army, far worse than Custer's defeat at Little Bighorn. Denny figured that of the 1,400 men who took part in the action, only 500 escaped uninjured. More than 630 men were either dead or missing. Of the 124 commissioned officers involved in the brief battle, 69 were dead, wounded, or missing.

Indian losses were twenty-one men killed and forty wounded.

Secretary of War Knox tried to reassure St. Clair that he had not done too badly. He wrote to the governor, "Your misfortune, to be sure, has been great and unexpected but, sir, it was one of those incidents which sometimes happen in human affairs, which could not, under existing circumstances have been prevented." He added, "[B]oth your reputation and the reputation of the troops under your command are unimpeached."

Knox was only partly right. President Washington flew into a fit of rage when he received the news of St. Clair's defeat. He stripped St. Clair of his military command but allowed him to stay on for a time as governor of the Northwest Territory. Perhaps Washington feared that too close an examination of St. Clair's failures would cast a poor light on the man who had appointed him: Washington himself. At any rate, the president prevented Congress from holding an inquiry into the disastrous campaign.

Despite Washington's partial protection, Americans realized that the campaign had been a fiasco, as reflected in the words of a poster printed in Boston:

A Horrid Fight there hap'd of late,
The Fourth Day of November,
When a Vast Number Met their Fate.
We all shall well remember,
"Twas over renown'd Ohio land,
And fatal prov'd of old,
Bad to relate! Our federal band,
Were slain by Indians bold!

Tecumseh, it is said, took no direct part in the fighting against St. Clair. His role was that of a scout. During St. Clair's long and ungainly march through the Ohio woods, Tecumseh commanded one of several parties that spied on the whites from the forest shadows and sent word of their whereabouts to Little Turtle and Blue Jacket. During the battle, Tecumseh's group was one of several scouting parties that watched the back trail in case additional troops, advancing from the rear, tried to reinforce St. Clair's men. Tecumseh and his band saw the fleeing soldiers and militiamen but did not reach the main battlefield until after the fighting was over. There they received a share of the captured weapons and equipment.

Jubilation was the mood in the Shawnee and Miami villages that winter. People lit victory fires and danced victory dances. After trouncing St. Clair's army, the frontier Indians believed that they could defend Ohio forever.

NOTES

p. 50   "My arm fails me . . ." Quoted in Bil Gilbert, *God Gave Us This Country* (New York: Atheneum, 1989), p. 107.

p. 51   "During the Indian wars . . ." Gilbert, p. 109.

pp. 52–53 "In several instances . . ." R. David Edmunds, *Tecumseh and the Quest for Indian Leadership* (Boston: Little, Brown, 1984), p. 27.

p. 53   "As to the lands . . ." Quoted in Sanford Wexler, *Westward Expansion: An Eyewitness History* (New York: Facts On File, 1991), p. 30.

p. 55   "the finest light . . ." James M. Perry, *Arrogant Armies: Great Military Disasters and the Generals Behind Them* (New York: John Wiley & Sons, 1996), p. 32.

p. 55   "undistinguished veteran . . ." and "a fondness for the bottle." Perry, p. 31.

p. 55   "one of the most disastrous . . ." Perry, p. 31.

p. 55   "no military genius." Perry, p. 37.

p. 55   "These were no ordinary . . ." Perry, pp. 34–35.

p. 56   "Venison . . ." and "cat fish . . ." Perry, p. 34.

p. 58   "convinced that he had won . . ." Perry, p. 41.

p. 58   "For God's sake . . ." Perry, p. 43.

p. 59   "Others knew better . . ." Perry, p. 46.

p. 59   "I expected little . . ." Perry, p. 46.

p. 59   "Harmar was a calamity . . ." Perry, p. 47.

pp. 59–60 "General St. Clair . . ." Quoted in Perry, p. 47.

pp. 60–61 "generally wanting the essential stamina . . ." Quoted in Perry, p. 50.

p. 61   "Girty brought the warriors . . ." Perry, p. 53.

p. 61   "You must go . . ." Quoted in Perry, p. 49.

p. 63   "Our prospects are gloomy . . ." Quoted in Perry, p. 54.

pp. 63–64 "the firing of the enemy . . ." Quoted in Perry, p. 54.

p. 64   "cowardly . . ." Quoted in Perry, p. 54.

p. 65   "When the Americans began counting . . ." Perry, p. 55.

p. 65   "Your misfortune . . ." Quoted in Perry, p. 58.

p. 66   "A Horrid fight . . ." Quoted in Perry, pp. 57–58.

FALLEN
TIMBERS
AND BEYOND

St. Clair's defeat caused an uproar in the United States. President Washington and Secretary of War Knox, convinced that all-out war with the Indians of the Northwest Territory was unavoidable, wanted to assemble a larger army and strike again quickly.

By and large, the American public did not share their eagerness. Many Americans had been shocked by the high cost of the Indian war, in both lives and money. Some spoke out against the endless fighting, saying that it was the responsibility of the United States, as an enlightened and civilized nation, to solve the problem without utterly wiping out the Indians. A substantial peace movement arose, and it put pressure on Congress. As a result, Congress told Washington and Knox that they could have the bigger army they wanted—but only if, before they went to war again, they made a serious effort to come to peace with the Indian tribes. Knox agreed to do so, admitting that an outright slaughter of the tribes might blot the new nation's history, triggering comparisons with the Spanish conquistadors of an earlier era. "If our modes of population and war destroy the tribes," he wrote, "the disinterested part of mankind and posterity will be apt to classify the effects of our conduct and that of the Spaniards in Mexico and Peru together."

The federal government therefore sent out commissioners with peace offers to the Ohio River valley in 1792. The Indians, buoyed by their recent victories, rejected the offers. Some of the rejections were quite definite: Indians caught the messengers carrying the offers and killed them as spies. One man who died this way was Hardin, the Kentucky colonel who had fared so poorly in the Harmar campaign.

By the summer of 1792 the federal government—acting through British agents and their contacts in the Iroquois Confederacy—had managed to arrange a peace conference with the western tribes. The conference took place in the Shawnee villages along the Auglaize River in northern Ohio. Nearly a thousand Indians from a dozen tribes attended. The U.S. government offered a compromise. It declared that if the Indians would give up the land east of the Muskingum River, the United States would allow them to keep the rest of Ohio. Led by the Shawnee, the tribes rejected this proposal and demanded the return of all Ohio lands.

Washington and Knox had not expected the peace overtures to succeed. They were busy building up the western army, which sorely needed strengthening. At the end of St. Clair's campaign, the army had had six forts west of the Appalachian Mountains and only 750 men. The War Department immediately began posting troops to the west. It also sent a number of new officers to the frontier. One of them was an eighteen-year-old ensign named William Henry Harrison. He arrived at Fort Washington not long after St. Clair's defeat and was not impressed with his fellow officers, most of whom he considered to be lazy drunkards.

Washington appointed a new commander in chief to oversee the rebuilding of the western army. His choice was Major General Anthony Wayne, a Revolutionary War veteran who was called "Mad Anthony." Wayne had earned this nickname not because of ferocity or craziness on the battlefield, but because once, when he had refused to acknowledge that he knew someone who had gotten into trouble, the disreputable acquaintance had exclaimed, "The man must be mad!"

Wayne had very definite ideas on the subjects of Indian peace and Indian war. He wrote to friends in the Senate, "Peace with the Indians is out of the question. The savages are stimulated by British emissaries to continue the war until the Ohio be made the

General "Mad" Anthony Wayne, whose nickname did *not* refer to his ferocity in battle, came to the Northwest to do what Harmar and St. Clair had failed to do: defeat the Indian confederacy. *(National Archives)*

boundary." He called the Indians "savages who have become confident, haughty, and insolent from reiterated success . . . and wanton and deliberate massacre." Wayne also had a plan for making war on the Indians. He rightly believed that he possessed more insight into their strengths and weaknesses than foolish

Harmar or overconfident St. Clair, both of whom had launched their campaigns in the fall. Wayne wrote to Knox, "I consider the Indian an enemy formidable only when he has a choice of time and ground. In the *fall* of the year he's strong, ferocious, and full of spirits—corn is in plenty and venison and other game everywhere to be met with; in the *Spring* he is half-starved, weak, and dispirited."

Tecumseh may have attended the 1792 peace conference, but he probably played little part in the negotiations. He was still a junior war leader, although he was increasingly accepted as a spokesperson for the tribe's younger, more aggressive warriors. Certainly he approved of the decision to reject the peace offer; he still believed with all his heart that Ohio belonged to the Indians.

While the U.S. government was trying to arrange peace and preparing for war, Tecumseh resumed the life of a roving Shawnee war chieftain. He led at least four raids against white settlers in 1792. In several of them he tangled with Simon Kenton, a Kentucky frontiersman whom the Indians regarded as one of the most dreaded of the Long Knives. Both times, Tecumseh and Kenton failed to kill one another. Once, when Tecumseh's men caught one of Kenton's rangers, the warriors killed the prisoner while Tecumseh was away from camp. According to Stephen Ruddell, when Tecumseh discovered what they had done he "was very angry telling them it was a cowardly act to kill a man who was tied." Incidents such as this forced even Tecumseh's enemies to feel a grudging respect for his highly developed sense of honor.

In the summer of 1793 representatives of the U.S. government met once more to discuss peace with chieftains from the Shawnee and other tribes. This time the meeting was held at Niagara-on-the-Lake in Ontario, Canada. The American agents repeated their earlier offer: In exchange for eastern Ohio, the United States would leave western Ohio alone. Indians and whites could share Ohio as peaceful neighbors. This time the agents added that if the Indians accepted the offer, the government would pay them a considerable sum into the bargain.

Some Indians were inclined to accept this offer. But the Shawnee were firmly against it, as were the Delaware. These tribes had just learned that their friends, the Creek, had been attacked by settlers in Georgia. Furthermore, they did not believe that the U.S. government sincerely wanted peace. Why had it sent a large new army to Fort Washington if not to attack the Indians?

With the encouragement of British agents who had acquired influence in the tribe through years of friendship, the Shawnee persuaded the other tribes to turn down the compromise. They wanted all of Ohio to remain Indian land, and they suggested that the government force the whites who had already settled in Ohio to leave. The government could pay them for the inconvenience with the money it had offered to the Indians. The federal representatives rejected this proposal.

The Shawnee were also encouraged in their defiance by the construction of a new British post called Fort Miami on the Maumee River, near where Toledo, Ohio, now stands. The Indians took the fort as a sign that their friends the British would stand by them if the Americans attacked. Lord Dorchester, the top British official in Canada, had recently made some bold statements about teaching the Americans a lesson, and the Indians took his words as further evidence that the British would support them. The Indians, however, did not know that the British government in London was not ready to challenge the United States openly. Dorchester had spoken without authority, and his statement had nothing to do with official British policy at the time.

Still, the Indians had rejected the American offer. The peace negotiations had failed. It was time to prepare for war. Wayne was ready. He wrote to Knox, "Give me authority to make these arrangements [to run the war as he wanted] and I will pledge my reputation as an officer to establish myself at the Miami villages, or at any other place that may be thought more proper, in the face of all the savages of the wilderness." Wayne also claimed that although the settlers and the War Department had long feared an alliance, or confederacy, among the tribes, the Indians were now at odds. The confederacy had failed to form, and Wayne did not believe that the tribes would cooperate with one another against him.

By June of 1794 Wayne had built two new forts—Fort Greenville and Fort Recovery—on the route between Fort Washington and the Maumee River. He had stocked these advance forts with supplies and ammunition, and he had marshaled a force of more than 3,500 men at Fort Greenville. The Indians, who had watched all of Wayne's moves closely, knew that he was ready to launch his attack northward. Tecumseh and other war leaders had sent messages to the other tribes. They had mustered between 1,500 and 1,800 troops from half a dozen Native American nations. This force was waiting north of Fort Recovery for Wayne to arrive.

Some of the Indians, including Tecumseh, became impatient while waiting for Wayne to leave Fort Greenville. Tecumseh joined a band of warriors from five tribes who attacked a supply train as it left Fort Recovery, hoping to capture some pack horses. The attack did not go as planned. While the Shawnee and Delaware in the party tried to secure the horses, the Great Lakes Indians—Ottawa, Potawatomi, and Chippewa warriors—decided on the spur of the moment to capture the fort. This proved impossible, for the fort was well defended, and finally

Wayne's troops built Fort Greenville in western Ohio as a base for their campaign. A decade later, ironically, Tecumseh's followers settled nearby. *(State Historical Society of Wisconsin, Whi(X3)40386, 5-1017)*

the attackers had to withdraw. As they marched northward to rejoin the main force, the Ottawa, Potawatomi, and Chippewa blamed the Shawnee and Delaware for not helping them. The Shawnee and Delaware replied that they had followed the original plan and that the others had acted wildly, endangering them all. After much bickering, 300 or so Ottawa, Potawatomi, and Chippewa fighters left the main Indian force and returned to their homes in Michigan. The withdrawal of so many warriors would hurt the Indians when they finally met Wayne.

Much heartened by the news he received from his spies about the departure of the Great Lakes Indians, Wayne was now marching north. He came to the Auglaize River and found the Shawnee and Miami villages deserted. After burning the villages and their cornfields, he led his men on to the junction of the Auglaize and Maumee rivers. There they built yet another stockade, Fort Defiance. From here Wayne sent messages to the Indians, asking them one last time if they would meet with him to make peace.

The Indians were far too committed to the war to consider making peace now. They had abandoned their villages, sent their women and children to safety in Michigan, and chosen a battle site. Little Turtle had been their principal war chieftain until he suggested that it might be wise to consider Wayne's offer of peace. Blue Jacket and Tecumseh questioned Little Turtle's courage and vowed to drive Wayne back to the Ohio River. Little Turtle resigned his leadership with dignity, and Blue Jacket became the principal chieftain of the Indian force, with Tecumseh as one of his top lieutenants.

The Indians had decided to make their stand at Fallen Timbers, so named after a storm knocked down many trees there. The war leaders felt that the timber on the ground would provide cover for them and would also slow the American advance. Once again, the Indians worked themselves up to fight—only to end up sitting and waiting. Wayne camped his army ten miles from Fallen Timbers and rested there for two days. During this time a thunderstorm drove many of the

Indians to seek shelter in the Indian camp that had grown around Fort Miami, the British post. When Wayne finally did advance to the site of the battle only about 400 warriors remained at their posts. Tecumseh was among them. So were his brothers Sauwauseekau and Lalawethika. The three of them were part of a Shawnee and Wyandot ambush party that was hidden in some bushes in front of the main Indian line.

Wayne had trained his troops well, and they were far more reliable than Harmar's and St. Clair's terrified militiamen. The soldiers advanced steadily, urged on by Wayne, who galloped up and down the line on his white horse, screaming that he would shoot any soldier who did not fight. When the Indians fired on these troops, they did not run but instead regrouped, reloaded, and marched forward. Before long the Indian line wavered, then broke. The warriors were retreating.

Tecumseh held his group together as long as he could, repeatedly firing on Wayne's lines to cover the retreat of the main force. Sauwauseekau was shot by return fire and fell dead. By then most of the warriors had fled the field and Tecumseh's little band was on the verge of being surrounded. To escape they broke from cover and attacked an American artillery squad, which included a horse-drawn cannon wagon. Cutting free the horses, they leaped astride them and pelted away, the last Indians to leave the field. The entire battle had lasted less than an hour.

The Americans had about 130 casualties, probably more than the Indians. Yet Fallen Timbers was clearly an American victory. It broke the Indians' morale and showed them that they were up against a dangerous opponent.

The battle itself was less disastrous, from the Indians' standpoint, than what happened after it. Writes Harry Emerson Wildes, Wayne's biographer:

> Politically speaking, the aftermath of Fallen Timbers was quite as important as the battle itself. Terror-stricken Indians . . . threw down their guns and ran to Fort Miami, seeking shelter. To their astonishment and

dismay, Major William Campbell, commander of the post, kept his gates tight shut. Blue Jacket, Little Turtle, and Tecumseh, the young war chief of the Shawnees, shouted for sanctuary, but Major Campbell paid no heed. The Indians knew now that their cause was hopeless, since their Father, the King of England, would not keep his promises. Wayne's task of making a peace treaty with the defeated tribes was thus assured.

Military historian James M. Perry believes that the Battle of Fallen Timbers was "the most lastingly significant battle fought by Native Americans." It was, Perry claims, the point of no return in the Indians' long struggle to retain their independence and their lands. He writes, "Plains Indians fought on into the middle of the nineteenth century, and these anticlimactic battles are better known to most Americans. But the sad fate of the American Indian had been decided years earlier, in the middle heartland of America."

At the time, of course, neither the Indians nor the whites saw the Battle of Fallen Timbers from the distant perspective of

This illustration accompanied an article about the Battle of Fallen Timbers that future president Theodore Roosevelt wrote for *Harper's Weekly* in 1896. *(Ohio Historical Society)*

history. The Indians knew simply that they had lost a battle, their villages, and the hope of British support. The Americans knew that their victory at Fallen Timbers had placed them in a position of strength. Now they could impose peace terms of their choosing on the defeated Indians.

"Mad Anthony" Wayne had won the battle, and "Mad Anthony" Wayne would make the peace. In the fall of 1794 his messengers told the tribes that the Americans were willing to make peace and that Wayne would meet with them the following summer.

By now the warriors from the Indiana, Michigan, and Illinois tribes had returned home. The Shawnee and Miami, however, had no homes to return to. Most of the Shawnee were living in refugee camps near the mouth of the Maumee River, along the shore of Lake Erie. They kept themselves separate from the Miami refugees, for relations between the two peoples had cooled after Blue Jacket's clash with Little Turtle.

The Shawnee were in a precarious state. The men had spent so much time preparing for war that they had done little hunting, and the women's fields had been destroyed in the fighting. Sympathetic British Indian agents gave the Shawnee supplies that helped them survive the winter.

Tecumseh, however, did not spend that winter at the refugee camp. He was angry at the British for Campbell's betrayal and refused to meet with or accept aid from the British agents. Grieving for Sauwauseekau and bitter than the war had gone awry, he withdrew into the forest with a few family members and friends and spent the winter in a small hunting camp.

When summer came, Wayne summoned the chieftains of the Northwest Territory tribes to Greenville and presented them with gifts and feasts. About 1,100 Indians—chieftains and their bodyguards—attended the council. In August, after several weeks of talks, they agreed to the harsh terms laid out by Wayne and the other American negotiators. Under the Treaty of Greenville, the United States received all but the northwestern third of Ohio and a large part of what is now Indiana. In addition, the

THE ROMANCE OF REBECCA

One of the many tales that became part of the Tecumseh mythology concerned the Galloway family of Ohio. James Galloway was a Kentucky pioneer who in 1797 crossed the Ohio River and settled his family in southern Ohio. At that time, in the grim years after the defeat of Fallen Timbers, Tecumseh was living in the region with his small band of family members and friends. Many years later, after James Galloway and Tecumseh were both long dead, Galloway's great-grandson published a book in which he recounted a family story about Tecumseh.

The Shawnee chieftain supposedly fell in love with Galloway's blue-eyed teenage daughter Rebecca, who called him "Mr. Tikomfa Chief." The two went for canoe rides together. Rebecca read the plays of William Shakespeare to her Indian suitor. According to the Galloway legend, Tecumseh's favorite play was *Hamlet*—the story of a prince who must overthrow an unjust usurper and restore his land to its rightful rule. It is easy to imagine Tecumseh seeing an echo of his own circumstances in Hamlet's situation.

Canoe rides and poetry deepened Tecumseh's ardor, and eventually he asked James Galloway for his daughter's hand in marriage. Galloway, who recognized Tecumseh's admirable qualities, replied that the decision was up to his daughter. Rebecca apparently returned Tecumseh's feelings. She told him that she believed they could be happy together but that she could only marry him if he left his people and dressed, worked, and lived like a white man. Sadly, Tecumseh told her that their marriage could not be, for he would never leave his people, but that he would always love her. Then he bade her farewell, never to see her again.

The "romance of Rebecca" is not quite as outlandish as the legend that Tecumseh was the grandson of the governor of South Carolina. Yet it is almost certainly just as untrue. Although Tecumseh may well have known the Galloways, there is no evidence that he had a relationship of any sort with their daughter. None of Tecumseh's white or Shawnee acquaintances—including people who knew him well and spent much time with him during these years—ever mentioned a romance with a white woman. The story of Rebecca Galloway is another example of how both Indians and whites embroidered Tecumseh's history in the years after his death, making him a larger-than-life figure like the hero of a popular novel.

In Howard Chandler Christy's *The Treaty of Greenville*, Little Turtle, chief of the Miami, hands a ceremonial belt to General Wayne. Background figures include William Henry Harrison, future explorers Meriwether Lewis and William Clark, and war leaders Blue Jacket and Black Hoof. *(Ohio Historical Society)*

Indians agreed that the new American forts in Indian territory could remain.

The Treaty granted the Indians a onetime payment of $20,000 worth of trade goods and annual payments of $500 to $10,000 per tribe. It also granted the Indians title to the lands west of the Treaty of Greenville line—as long as they remained at peace.

Despite the fact that the Treaty of Greenville gave the Shawnee homeland in southern Ohio to the whites, the Shawnee chieftain Blue Jacket was one of the first to sign. He despised the whites, but he believed that the Indians had nothing to gain by further fighting. Blue Jacket would spend the coming years drinking and spending a secret allowance he received from the government each year as a reward for signing the treaty. He would be replaced as principal chieftain of the Shawnee by Black Hoof.

Little Turtle of the Miami was the last and most reluctant of 91 chiefs to make his mark on the Treaty of Greenville, even though the Americans had promised to build him a fine house near what is now Fort Wayne, Indiana. When Little Turtle signed the treaty, he said that he would be the last to break it. He kept his word. During the remaining fifteen years of his life he never again made war on the whites. Believing that it was useless for the Indians to resist the advance of American civilization, Little Turtle spent the rest of his life urging the Indians to adopt American-style agriculture and live in peace with the whites. He thought it was best for the Indians to try to fit in, or assimilate, to American society. Perhaps Little Turtle saw more clearly than many Indian leaders the sad fate that lay in store for his people. Or perhaps, as Tecumseh believed, he simply gave up too easily.

Tecumseh refused to go to Greenville. He did not want to make peace—not on the terms that the Americans were forcing on the Indians. To Tecumseh, southern Ohio was still Indian territory and still his home. He had nothing but scorn for the chieftains who signed the Treaty of Greenville. In Tecumseh's opinion, these "government chiefs" had betrayed their own people for a few dollars and some fancy trinkets—or because they were afraid to keep fighting. Even men such as Little Turtle and Black Hoof lost honor in Tecumseh's eyes. "Dogs and skunks have not so little mind as those who did this," Tecumseh said of the chieftains who signed the treaty. "Every Indian who has put his thumb to it should have his thumb cut off!"

Above all, Tecumseh did not feel himself bound to obey the treaty. He had not signed it, and those who had signed it did not represent him. In the years to come, many Indians would realize that the Treaty of Greenville had not been good for their people. Members of many tribes would respect Tecumseh because he alone, of all the notable leaders, had refused to sign the treaty. In the eyes of young warriors especially, Tecumseh's refusal set him apart from the chieftains who had groveled or knuckled under to the whites. Tecumseh would become a symbol of Native American pride, spirit, and independence.

According to the Treaty of Greenville, Indians could hunt in southern Ohio until the region was fully settled, but they could not live there. Tecumseh defied the treaty even before it was signed; by May of 1795 he had led his band of a hundred or so followers south to a region called Deer Creek, where a number of white settlers were living. There the Shawnee tried to recapture their prewar way of life. They found an old Shawnee settlement, cleared the fields, and planted corn. In the fall they hunted deer but found that game was much scarcer than it used to be. War and the growth of white settlements had made life hard for the wild creatures of the woods as well as for the Shawnee. In spring 1796 Tecumseh led his band to the site of another former Shawnee village on the Miami River. He had returned to the scene of his boyhood.

By now Tecumseh was twenty-eight years old. He was about five feet and ten inches tall, a bit taller than the average Shawnee, and many of those who knew him described him as muscular and very vigorous. Tecumseh embodied all of the qualities of a traditional Shawnee leader. He was a brilliant, spellbinding orator. He was a warrior of unquestioned courage. He also had a gentle side and a strong sense of responsibility; his fellow Shawnee noted he was "kind and attentive to the aged and infirm, looking personally to their comfort, repairing their wigwams when winter approached, giving them skins for moccasins and clothing, and sharing with them the choicest game which the woods and seasons afforded."

During the mid-1790s Tecumseh married, apparently twice. Details and dates are vague. Most sources say that he married his first wife in 1794 or 1795. Although she bore him a son, the marriage was not a success, for the woman proved to be bossy and ill-tempered. Tecumseh divorced her and sent his son to live with his sister Tecumpease.

In 1796 Tecumseh married again, perhaps because his followers convinced him that a mature war leader should be married. His second wife, Mamate, was a warrior's widow who was somewhat older than Tecumseh. She, too, bore Tecumseh a son. This boy's name was Pachetha. Mamate seems to have disappeared from Tecumseh's life by 1800, but historians do not know whether she died or the marriage simply ended. Like his older brother, Pachetha became part of the Tecumpease's household.

Tecumseh is said to have lived with women from time to time during the next decade. As far as is known, however, he never married again or fathered more children. Judging from the historical record, Tecumseh had little contact with the sons who lived with Tecumpease. While they were growing up, their father was busy pursuing a dream of his own.

NOTES

p. 68   "If our modes..." Quoted in Harry Emerson Wildes, *Anthony Wayne: Trouble Shooter of the American Revolution* (New York: Harcourt, Brace, and Co., 1941), p. 360.

pp. 69–70 "Peace with the Indians..." Quoted in Wildes, p. 360.

p. 70   "savages who have become confident..." Quoted in Wildes, p. 364.

p. 71   "I consider the Indian..." Quoted in Wildes, pp. 364–365.

p. 71   "was very angry..." Quoted in Bil Gilbert, *God Gave Us This Country* (New York: Atheneum, 1989), p. 161.

p. 72   "Give me authority..." Quoted in Wildes, p. 365.

pp. 75–76 "Politically speaking..." Wildes, p. 464.

p. 76   "the most lastingly..." James M. Perry, *Arrogant Armies: Great Military Disasters and the Generals Behind Them* (New York: John Wiley & Sons, 1996), p. 59.

p. 76   "Plains Indians fought on..." Perry, p. 59.

p. 80   "Dogs and skunks..." Quoted in Robert Cwiklik, *Tecumseh* (New York: Chelsea House, 1993), p. 60.

p. 81   "kind and attentive..." Quoted in R. David Edmunds, *Tecumseh and the Quest for Indian Leadership* (Boston: Little, Brown, 1984), pp. 43–44.

THE SHAWNEE PROPHET

6

I n 1797 Tecumseh led his people away from southern Ohio to an area where there were fewer white settlers. The small band of Shawnee migrated west into eastern Indiana, settling near the Whitewater River. A few years later Tecumseh received an offer from a group of Delaware who had settled in Indiana after being driven out of their homeland in eastern Ohio. These Delaware lived along the White River, north of present-day Indianapolis, and they invited Tecumseh's Shawnee band to join them there. The Shawnee built a new village next to the Delaware villages. This White River community was to be Tecumseh's home base until 1805, although he traveled frequently.

Tecumseh had acquired a reputation for levelheadedness and eloquence among both whites and other Shawnee leaders. People often turned to him for help in resolving questions or settling disputes. The dignity and wisdom with which he did so commanded the respect of both races.

In 1799, Tecumseh was one of several Shawnee chieftains who met with settlers in southern Ohio to calm their fears about Shawnee hunters in what was by then white territory. Some of the whites who were there later reported that Tecumseh spoke with "force and eloquence."

In 1803 white officials again asked Tecumseh to return to southern Ohio. Fighting had broken out along the Scioto River. A homesteader had been murdered. In revenge, a group of local whites killed an elderly Shawnee man who had had nothing to do with the murder. Now settlers in the area were afraid of a large

Indian uprising. Farmers abandoned their homesteads and sought refuge in Chillicothe, the town built on the former site of the Shawnee settlement Chalahgawtha.

Tecumseh went to Chillicothe and told the frontierspeople not to fear an Indian war. The Shawnee, he said, intended to live in peace. The old man who was killed had managed to kill one of his attackers before dying, so the Shawnee had no desire for further revenge. Everyone could go home without fear. Although no record exists of Tecumseh's speech on this occasion, a militia captain present said that Tecumseh was "one of the most dignified men I ever beheld." The Shawnee chieftain's "noble bearing dispelled as if by magic the apprehensions of the whites." The settlers' panic subsided, the crisis passed, and Tecumseh returned to the White River to ponder his people's future.

The first years of the 19th century were a stressful time for the Indians of the Old Northwest. Many people had been dispossessed, or removed from their lands, by the Treaty of Greenville. They had to migrate into unfamiliar territories, sometimes encroaching on other tribes. The aftermath of the Treaty of Greenville created many new relationships among the tribes. Some of these new relationships were alliances and fusions, like the Shawnee-Delaware community at White River. Other relationships, however, deteriorated into rivalry and friction as the Native American nations struggled to adjust themselves to the changes that were sweeping over the Old Northwest.

Some of these changes affected the Indians' basic livelihood. It became increasingly harder for them to find enough game to feed themselves. As the line of settlement advanced west and north, the Long Knives ranged farther and farther into the forest to hunt. They took a considerable amount of game from territory that was supposed to belong to the Indians.

One white official who recognized the hardship that white hunters caused to the Indians was William Henry Harrison. After serving as one of Wayne's aides at the Battle of Fallen Timbers, Harrison had been the secretary of the Northwest Territory for several years. In 1801 Congress made him governor of the newly created Indiana Territory. At his headquarters in Vincennes, Harrison listened to the complaints of Indians who claimed that the Long Knives were crossing the Treaty of Greenville line to hunt. Admitting that the white hunters were wastefully violating the Indian hunting grounds, Harrison wrote:

> The people of Kentucky living on the Ohio from the mouth of the Kentucky river down to the Mississippi make a constant practice of crossing over onto the Indian lands opposite to them every fall to kill deer, bear, and buffaloe—the latter from being in great abundance a few years ago is now scarcely to be met with. One white hunter will destroy more game than five of the common Indians—the latter generally contenting himself with a sufficiency for present subsistence—while the other eager after game hunt for the skin of the animal alone.

Yet Harrison could not or would not punish the offenders. In truth, the federal government had little interest in supporting the claims of Indians against whites. Many in the government believed that it would be best if the Indians found life so hard that they just kept moving west, away from Indiana and Illinois—territories that settlers were already eyeing hungrily.

Game animals were not the only creatures that were becoming scarce in the Old Northwest. Fur-bearing animals were also less numerous than they had once been. Unfortunately, the Indians were increasingly dependent upon the fur trade. Their self-sufficiency had been eroded by years of fighting and dislocation. Now they bought goods from traders or frontier merchants. When the fur harvest was poor, the Indians made their purchases on credit, often falling deeply into debt. They had become part of an economic system that they did not control.

The fur trade affected the Indians' cultural as well as their economic lives. In the hope of getting enough furs to meet their needs, men began hunting farther away from their home villages and staying away for longer periods of time. These prolonged absences weakened the ties that held families and communities together. The Shawnee, for example, had to change, postpone, or omit some of their traditional seasonal rituals. In addition, although Shawnee women had always been free to choose their own partners, now some women and girls had become prostitutes, selling sex for money, goods, or alcohol.

Alcohol continued to ravage the tribes, further destabilizing family and community ties. Visitors to Shawnee villages during these years reported much alcoholism and frequent drunken binges and brawls. Some historians have suggested that the Northwest Territory Indians were especially vulnerable to alcohol at this time because Fallen Timbers and Greenville had thrown many of them into states of depression. Uncertain of their future, out of touch with their past, the Indians turned to liquor as a source of temporary pleasure and forgetfulness. Some Indian leaders saw the evils of alcohol and begged the territorial authorities to keep the whiskey peddlers out of the Indian villages, with armed troops if necessary. The whiskey trade was illegal, but it was so widespread and so well-established that officials could not have stopped it without a major military law-enforcement campaign, which they were not willing to make.

Along with alcoholism, disease was on the rise among the tribes. Contact with whites had always exposed the Native Americans to such illnesses as measles, smallpox, and influenza, but now more Indians were living closer to more whites than ever before. In addition, the Indians' way of life had become less healthy. Villages and camps were crowded. Trade supplies and alcohol formed a diet considerably less nutritious than the traditional Indian diet. Diseases spread more rapidly and were more deadly among a weakened population.

Amid these dire conditions, knowing in their hearts that the relentless tide of whites would keep rolling westward, some Indians believed that their best hope for the future was to join that tide. They decided to adapt to white society. As historian R. David Edmunds writes, "Convinced that their traditional way of life no longer could cope with the changes swirling around them, some Shawnees decided to walk the white man's road." One chieftain who made that choice was Black Hoof. Under his leadership, most of the Shawnee who still lived in western Ohio had settled on the Auglaize and the upper Miami rivers in an area they called Wapakoneta. They asked the government for farm implements and for someone to teach them white agricultural methods. From now on, decreed Black Hoof, they would live in permanent homes, raise livestock, and try to live as the whites did. To the west, Little Turtle urged the Miami of Fort Wayne along the same path. These and other Indian leaders favored assimilation, or acculturation, which meant adopting white values and ways of life.

Other Native Americans sought a different path. They turned to their spiritual beliefs for some explanation of what had happened to them. They saw the world as a battleground for a cosmic war between the forces of good and evil—or, in terms of the Shawnee mythology, between the Master of Life and the Great Serpent. The Great Serpent was connected with water, and some Shawnee called the whites, who had come to North America over the sea, his children. The Great Serpent also had servants among the Indians, witches who worked evil magic on the tribes. Now that the white people were so numerous and powerful, some Indians believed, the witches' magic was growing stronger.

Still, perhaps the Master of Life would yet defeat the Great Serpent. A few Shawnee explained this belief to government officials in Indiana. They told tribal tales about how the first white people had stolen knowledge from the Shawnee. The whites had then appeared on the Atlantic shore in a strange vessel like nothing the Indians had seen before:

> At first [the Indians] took it for a great bird, but they
> soon found it to be a monstrous canoe filled with the
> very people who had got the knowledge which be-
> longed to the Shawnees. After these white people had
> landed, they were not content with having the knowl-
> edge which belonged to the Shawnees, but they usurped
> their land also. They pretended, indeed, to have pur-
> chased these lands but the very goods they gave for
> them were more the property of the Indians than of the
> white people, because the knowledge which enabled

> them to manufacture these goods actually belonged to
> the Shawnees. But these things will soon end. The Mas-
> ter of Life is about to restore to the Shawnees their
> knowledge and their rights and he will trample the
> Long Knives under his feet.

Their remarks showed that not all of the Indians had given in to despair or set their feet on the white man's road. Some believed that a new day was about to dawn for the tribes.

In this chaotic time of misery, change, and hope, a powerful new voice was heard in the land. It came from the unlikeliest source imaginable: Tecumseh's younger brother Lalawethika.

As many historians have noted, Lalawethika was in some ways Tecumseh's opposite. Tecumseh was an example of every Shawnee virtue. Lalawethika, one of the two survivors of the triplets born after Puckeshinwa's death, was an embarrassment to his people—during the earlier part of his life, at least.

As a child, Lalawethika was fat, oafish, and poor at games. His lack of agility and athletic skill made him a laughingstock among the Shawnee, who considered games very important. Unlike other boys, who could hardly wait to get their first weapons and start hunting, Lalawethika disliked hunting. He would rather stay in the village than go into the forest. He was clumsy with weap-ons—so much so that he put out his right eye with an arrow. Perhaps as an attempt to make up for these shortcomings or to attract attention, Lalawethika became loud and boastful. His brag-ging, aggressive personality, however, inspired annoyance rather than admiration. Even his older brothers Chiksika and Tecumseh generally ignored him.

Lalawethika seemed no more successful as an adult. He discov-ered alcohol in his teens and became an enthusiastic drinker. He did not participate in raids against the Long Knives, and when the Long Knives attacked the Shawnee villages, he hid in the forest with the women and children. Although he married, he was unable to provide for his family and depended on food and other handouts from Tecumseh.

As far as is known, Lalawethika's first battle came when he was twenty years old. He accompanied Tecumseh's band of fighters to Fallen Timbers. After the battle he attached himself to his older brother and became part of the band that followed Tecumseh to southern Ohio and then to Indiana. The other Shawnee warriors neither liked nor respected Lalawethika, but they tolerated him because he was Tecumseh's brother.

Lalawethika had a difficult time in White River. The community lived by hunting, and he was still a poor hunter. Although other people gave meat to his family, the ridicule Lalawethika endured drove him even further into alcoholism. Unable or unwilling to become a warrior, Lalawethika needed a way to earn respect. He decided to carve out a niche for himself in society by becoming a healer. An elderly shaman, or medicine man, named Penagashea lived in the village. Although Penagashea did not think much of Lalawethika, the younger man persuaded the shaman to take him on as an apprentice. Over the next couple of years Penagashea shared with Lalawethika some methods of the traditional Shawnee art of healing. He taught Lalawethika how to use charms, incantations, and medicines made from plants to cure various ailments.

After Penagashea died in 1804, Lalawethika considered himself the village shaman. The other Shawnee, however, still did not much like him, and many doubted his ability to heal. That ability was put to the test in 1805, when an influenza epidemic swept through the community. Lalawethika tried to cure the sick, but with little success. People died despite his efforts. (There was probably little that any shaman could have done to halt this deadly and highly contagious disease.) The epidemic proved a serious setback to Lalawethika's dreams of respect. The would-be shaman took to drinking more heavily than before this calamity and passed long hours brooding in his wigwam.

One night in 1805, Lalawethika had just lit his pipe when he fell to the floor unconscious. He remained that way for hours. His wife called the neighbors, and by morning they decided that he was

THE WAY OF THE SHAMAN

When Tecumseh's brother Lalawethika decided to become a shaman, he was attempting to fill a very important role in Native American society. Whites called Indian shamans "medicine men" because they were healers, but in the eyes of the Indians they were much more.

The Indians believed that shamans possessed the ability to communicate with spirits—both good spirits and evil ones. The shaman was therefore supposed to act as an intermediary, or go-between, between the human world and the world of spirits. Shamans interpreted dreams, unraveling the meanings of these messages sent from the spirit world to the dreamer. Using their own magical powers, shamans protected their communities against the wicked magic of demons, sorcerors, and witches. They guided people in ceremonies, including sacred dances and funerals, that were designed to please the spirits or communicate with them.

Magical beliefs and practical knowledge came together in the shaman's work as a healer. The chants, charms, and rituals that the shaman prescribed or performed to help a sick person were thought to have magical powers. Traditional folk medicine incorporating the local flora and fauna was another of the shaman's medical tools.

Shamans were skilled in the use of plants and herbs. They knew that certain snakeroots were effective in treating snakebites. They made cough syrup from the ground-up bark of wild cherry trees. They cleaned wounds with a liquid made from oak bark, which contains a chemical called tannin that reduces bleeding. They knew that the bark, roots, or leaves of certain kinds of willow trees yielded medicines for pain and fever; modern scientists know that willows contain salicylic acid, from which aspirin is made. In short, the shaman possessed a large body of practical herb lore that was passed from generation to generation. Unfortunately for Lalawethika—and for thousands of Indians—even the most carefully prepared remedies could not cure the deadly new diseases, such as influenza, brought to North America by the whites.

dead. While they were getting ready for the funeral, Lalawethika moved and spoke; he was not dead after all.

Lalawethika told the villagers of the strange and wonderful experience he had undergone. His soul had traveled to the world of spirits, and he had met the greatest of all spirits, the Master of Life. The Master of Life had carried him to a mountaintop from which he had seen a heavenly valley, filled with game and corn-fields. This, he was told, was the paradise of Indian souls. Those who remained virtuous and faithful to the Master of Life would have a happy and easy existence there. The souls of those who departed from the Master of Life's rules, however, would find themselves being tortured in a fiery wigwam.

What did the Master of Life want the Indians to do? The Master of Life, said Lalawethika, wanted the Indians to give up all things and habits they had acquired from the whites, whom the Master of Life hated. To enter the paradise of the virtuous, the Indians must wear skins instead of woven cloth. They must eat game, not live-stock, and corn, not wheat. They must hunt with bows and arrows, not guns, although Lalawethika said that the Master of Life would allow them to use guns against the whites. Above all, they must stop drinking alcohol, the white man's poison. Lalawethika then told his astonished audience that he would never touch another drop of liquor. He had been sent back to earth, he said, to carry the Master of Life's message to all the tribes. The Master had given him a new name: Tenskwatawa, which meant "The Open Door."

In the months that followed, Tenskwatawa entered several more trances. After each trance he was able to explain the Master of Life's message in greater detail.

The heart of the message was that the Indians had lost touch with their traditions. Their rituals and customs were falling into disuse. Drunkenness, violence, prostitution, and greed were de-stroying their culture. The Master of Life, said Tenskwatawa, wanted the Indians to treat each other as brothers and sisters. They should stop quarreling, be kind to one another, and show special reverence to the elderly, who were closer to the old ways. Indians should marry only Indians. No one should strive to hoard private property; instead, people should share with one another in a communal society, as the Shawnee used to do.

Tenskwatawa said that the Master of Life hated the Americans because they had been created by an evil spirit. The Indians should not try to copy the Americans' way of life. Furthermore, the Indians should begin to cut off their dealings with Americans. If

Tecumseh's hopeless younger brother transformed himself into Tenskwatawa and became known as the Shawnee Prophet, leader of a religious revival that went hand in hand with Tecumseh's political goals. *(Indiana Historical Society, negative C546)*

they needed guns, they should obtain them from the French or the British. Tenskwatawa also warned that evil witches were at work among the tribes, turning people against the Master of Life. Some of these witches were disguised as shamans or chieftains, such as those who urged their followers to become assimilated or acculturated into white society. Finally, Tenskwatawa presented new chants, songs, and rituals that he said had been designed by the Master of Life to replace old, worn-out ceremonies. According to Tenskwatawa, the Master of Life had promised that if the Indians followed his rules, "I will overturn the land, so that all the white people will be covered and you alone shall inhabit the land."

As word of these revelations spread, Indians began coming to hear them. They came at first from neighboring villages, then from farther away. Tenskwatawa, once a lazy and useless drunkard, now appeared to be not just a reformed man but a holy man. He attracted believers and followers. Soon he was known as the Prophet, or the Shawnee Prophet.

For years scholars and historians have debated the true nature of the Prophet's revelations, as well as the relationship between Tenskwatawa and Tecumseh. Before Lalawethika's transformation into Tenskwatawa, Tecumseh had been attracting followers who admired his resistance to the Treaty of Greenville and his refusal to assimilate. Most of these followers were young warriors, although there were a few older men and families. They came not just from the Shawnee tribe but from other Indian nations as well. They were seeking someone or something to give them hope and a sense of purpose.

The doctrines of Tenskwatawa, the Shawnee Prophet, filled that need. They also fit nicely with Tecumseh's views about how the Shawnee should be living. The Prophet encouraged the Indians to resist and reject the whites. He told his followers that their spiritual salvation depended on returning to their former way of life. Whatever Tecumseh's spiritual views, he certainly believed that the sheer physical survival of the Shawnee lay in such a return to tradition. In addition, the Prophet's message appealed to all the Indians of the region, not just the Shawnee. This aspect no doubt attracted

Native Americans from many tribes pledged their loyalty to the Prophet—and to Tecumseh, shown standing behind Tenskwatawa. *(Photo by C/Z HARRIS from Library of Congress collection)*

Tecumseh, who was forever searching for ways to pull people from the different tribes together.

Did Tecumseh create the "Master of Life" messages and convince his brother to deliver them, as some historians have suggested? Or did Lalawethika come up with the idea on his own and fake his trance, reinventing himself as a holy man in order to gain the respect that had eluded him all his life? Or did Lalawethika genuinely believe that during his coma he had spoken with the Master of Life and seen a vision of paradise?

There is no way to know the true story behind these occurrences. But whatever the source of the Prophet's message, he found many willing listeners. In times of oppression and upheaval, people turn eagerly to messiahs and reformers who promise to right wrongs and bring order out of chaos. Sometimes these reformers launch crusades that are both religious and political; this was certainly the case with Tenskwatawa. From the time of his first trance, the Prophet worked closely with Tecumseh, who had much to do with directing the movement that developed from his brother's teachings. Although he enthusiastically supported the Prophet's ideas, Tecumseh seems never to have stated in public or private whether or not he accepted the trances and messages from the spirit world as genuine. Tecumseh's spiritual beliefs, like so much else about this enigmatic leader, are a mystery.

Some scholars have suggested that the Shawnee Prophet was nothing more than Tecumseh's mouthpiece or puppet. There is no evidence that this was so, although it was clear on several occasions when the two men disagreed that Tecumseh dominated and outranked his brother. Other historians believe that the Prophet independently began a religious movement that the more powerful and eloquent Tecumseh took over and adapted to his own purposes. Again, there is no way to prove or disprove this theory.

For the most part, the two men appear to have cooperated. Together they encouraged the growth of a movement that was part religious revival, part political resistance. Tenskwatawa was a rising spiritual leader. Tecumseh soon called the tribes to action.

NOTES

p. 83   "force and eloquence." Quoted in R. David Edmunds, *Tecumseh and the Quest for Indian Leadership* (Boston: Little, Brown, 1984), p. 84.

p. 84   "one of the most . . ." and "noble bearing . . ." Quoted in Robert Cwiklik, *Tecumseh* (New York: Chelsea House, 1993), p. 58.

p. 85   "The people of Kentucky . . ." Quoted in Edmunds, p. 64.

p. 86   "Convinced that their . . ." Edmunds, p. 67.

pp. 87–88 "At first . . ." Quoted in Edmunds, p. 72.

p. 93   "I will overturn . . ." Quoted in Edmunds, p. 79.

TECUMSEH'S GRAND PLAN

In 1805 the Prophet and Tecumseh moved their growing community of followers back to Ohio. They built a village near Greenville, where, said Tenskwatawa, the Master of Life had ordered him to live. Perhaps the Master of Life wanted the Prophet to show his disregard for the Treaty of Greenville by taking up residence in the very place where the treaty had been signed—a place where, according to the treaty, no new Indian settlements could be founded. The Prophet and Tecumseh declared that because they had not agreed to the treaty, they were free to live in any part of Ohio if they chose. Government officials took no immediate action against the Shawnee brothers, but they kept a close eye on their activities.

The Prophet devoted himself to traveling and giving sermons, spreading the word that if the Indians followed the Master's ways, the whites would be cast down and the Indians would have their land back. The number of converts continued to rise as people from the Shawnee, Wyandot, Delaware, and Potawatomi tribes joined the Prophet's following. Tecumseh and the other senior men of the community handled the day-to-day government of the growing village.

In 1806 the Prophet's crusade became a witch hunt. Tenskwatawa visited Delaware villages in Indiana and identified four "witches." The Delaware killed them. The Prophet did the same thing in Wyandot villages in northern Ohio. Only the opposition of a powerful chieftain prevented four old Wyandot women from being executed as witches. The executions angered Tecumseh;

some sources say that he threatened to kill his brother if the witch hunts continued.

The witch hunts also outraged William Henry Harrison. From Vincennes Harrison sent a message to the Delaware. It was both a warning and a challenge:

> Who is this pretended prophet who dares to speak in the name of the Great Creator? Examine him. Is he more wise or virtuous than you are yourselves, that he should be selected to convey to you the orders of your God? Demand of him some proofs at least of his being the messenger of the Deity. If God has employed him he has doubtless authorized him to perform some miracles, that he may be known and received as a prophet. If he is really a prophet, ask of him to cause the sun to stand still—the moon to alter its course—or the dead to rise from their graves. If he does these things, you may then believe that he has been sent by God.

But Harrison's scornful challenge backfired.

The Prophet announced that he would make the sun stand still on June 16. A huge crowd gathered at Greenville to witness the miracle. The sun was high in the sky. Then Tenskwatawa raised his hand. Darkness slowly covered the sun. The summer day turned as gray as dusk. Many long minutes later, the darkness withdrew and the sun slowly reappeared. The Prophet had indeed "stopped" the sun.

Somehow Tenskwatawa had learned the date and time of a solar eclipse. The eclipse had certainly been discussed in Ohio, for several astronomers had recently visited the area and spoken of the coming celestial event. The whites who witnessed the "miracle" realized that it was a predictable solar phenomenon. For the Indians an eclipse was nothing new either. But Tenskwatawa's seeming ability to control the eclipse made a deep impression. Word of the Prophet's powers spread rapidly, bringing him converts from the Kickapoo and Great Lakes tribes.

Some of these converts were armed warriors, and their tone was decidedly militant. Antiwhite sentiment was spattered throughout their prayers, sermons, and speeches. White settlers in the area—and also the acculturated Shawnee at Wapakoneta and the Miami at Fort Wayne—grew jittery. Were Tecumseh and the Prophet going to start a new war? In the spring of 1807 representatives of the government told the Shawnee brothers that they had to leave Greenville. Tecumseh, who had by now become the movement's principal spokesman, refused, saying that the Master of Life had "appointed this place for us to light our fires, and here we will remain."

Tension rose that summer. Rumors of an Indian war spread through Ohio after a settler was murdered. And there were rumors of another war—a war with the British. Great Britain was still smarting from the loss of its American colonies thirty years earlier. At sea, British naval captains were in the habit of seizing American vessels, kidnapping their crews, and forcing the American seamen to work on British ships; the Americans, not unnaturally, resented these assaults. A British and an American ship exchanged shots in June 1807, sparking fears that war was imminent. And if the United States went to war with Britain, reasoned the settlers, surely the Indians would enter the war on the side of their former British allies. The frontier would be red with blood.

Once again Tecumseh rose to the task of calming people's fears. He was one of several Indian leaders who traveled to Chillicothe to meet with government officials. Tecumseh was the Indians' foremost speaker during the weeklong talks. His most important speech was open to the public, and although no record of Tecumseh's words exists, those who were there described his three-hour speech as "bold, commanding, and impassioned."

The Chillicothe speech marked an important turning point in Tecumseh's career. For the first time he spoke at length and publicly to a white audience about a topic that had occupied his thoughts for years: the Indians and their land.

Tecumseh started out by reviewing the treaties that Indians and whites had made in the past. He argued that the treaties were not valid because the chiefs who had signed them did not represent all Indians. Nevertheless, said Tecumseh, those treaties had come into being, and white people had moved into the former Indian

Little Turtle, once a war leader against the Americans, eventually decided that signing treaties and accepting government handouts was better than fighting. Tecumseh despised his former ally and the other "government chiefs." *(Indiana Historical Society, negative C2582)*

territories. Because this was so, the Indians would let the wrongful treaties stand. They would not try to force the settlers who had already moved into Kentucky and Ohio to leave. They would live at peace with their white neighbors. But the treaty-making must now stop. The Indians would give up no more land. And if the whites tried to take the Indians' remaining territories, the Indians would fight to the death to keep them.

Behind Tecumseh's speech lay an idea that had been forming for some time. He had developed a new concept of land ownership that was as different from the traditional Native American attitude toward the land as it was from the European-American concept. In traditional Indian thinking, land was "shared by all men but owned by none." People *used* the land, but the Indians lacked the concept of a claim or title to a particular piece of land, much less of a claim or title that could be bought, sold, or inherited. The Europeans and Americans, on the other hand, had based much of their culture and economy on the concept of private ownership of specific, measured, mapped parcels of land. Tecumseh's idea fell somewhere between these two positions.

His notion was that there was such a thing as "Indian land," and that it had a defined border that could be shown on a map. To this extent he had embraced the concept of ownership. Historian R. David Edmunds explains, however, that Tecumseh believed that "all the remaining Indian land belonged to no particular tribe, only to all the Indians in general. Therefore individual tribes no longer had the right to sell their territories to the government. If such sales should take place, they would require the consent of all the Indians. Of course this permission would be almost impossible to obtain."

Closely tied to this concept of common ownership was Tecumseh's vision of a new kind of Indian organization. He envisioned a confederation, or political and military union, that would bring *all* the tribes together, not just those whose languages were similar or who shared a history of alliances. Undoubtedly Tecumseh saw himself as the logical leader of such a confederation, but the idea itself grew out of much more than a desire for personal power. He was convinced that only by negotiating with one voice—and, if necessary, fighting as one army—could the Indian nations hope to resist further expansion by the whites.

Resistance and unity were more necessary than ever. In 1803 President Thomas Jefferson had sent Governor Harrison a long letter outlining his views on the fate of the Indians. Jefferson wanted to turn the Indians from nomadic hunters into farmers and weavers on fixed plots of land. Once the Indians were established on farms, they could be made to sell off their excess forest land. The plan worked in the other direction, too. Once the Indians had sold off their hunting grounds, they would have no choice but to assimilate and become farmers.

Following Jefferson's instructions, Harrison went about buying land on the Indian side of the Greenville line, even though the line was supposed to have been a permanent boundary between white and Indian territories. By 1807 Harrison had obtained 70 million

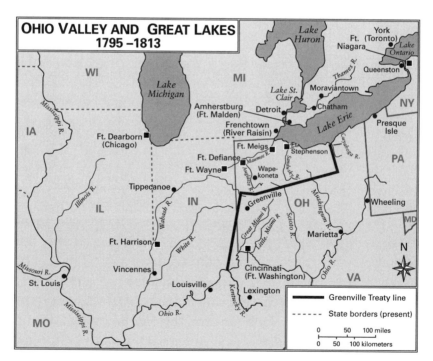

This map shows both the advance of white settlement into Indiana and Ohio and the places connected with Tecumseh's final military campaign.

acres of land in northern Ohio, Indiana, southern Michigan, Illinois, Missouri, and Wisconsin. He acquired these tracts through treaties with Ottawa, Wyandot, Delaware, Potawatomi, Chippewa, Miami, and Kaskaskia chieftains.

To Tecumseh, these treaties were meaningless, and the men who had signed them were contemptible "government chiefs" who had betrayed all Indians. The treaties angered many young warriors, some of whom joined Tecumseh and the Prophet at Greenville. These young men shared Tecumseh's vision of intertribal unity. Many older Indians, however, did not favor an intertribal confederation. They had no intention of giving up their own positions of leadership or of allying themselves with tribes that were their long-time enemies. Tecumseh knew that in order to bring the confederation into being he would have to win the support of some respected older leaders among the tribes.

First, however, it was time to leave Greenville. At the invitation of Main Poc, a Potawatomi chieftain, Tecumseh and the Prophet moved to Potawatomi territory. There they would be farther from the white government and closer to the western tribes, such as the Kickapoo, who were providing many of the new recruits for their movement. In the spring of 1808 Tecumseh, the Prophet, and their followers settled at the junction of the Wabash and Tippecanoe rivers in what is now northwestern Indiana.

The Shawnee brothers called their new home Prophetstown. It was to be not only the center of the Prophet's religion but also the capital of the hoped-for Indian confederacy. The village consisted of rows of bark wigwams, a medicine lodge, a council lodge, and an enormous log structure called the House of the Stranger, built to house visitors and converts.

While the Prophet and his followers were building Prophetstown, Tecumseh set off on the first of many journeys that would carry him across much of eastern North America. This time he went to Canada. British officials there sounded him out about the possibilities of an alliance in case of war with the United States. Remembering the betrayal at Fort Miami, Tecumseh said that he would be willing to help the British, but only if they made firm promises that they in turn would help the Indians.

The inhabitants of Prophetstown endured a grim winter in 1808 to 1809. They nearly starved, despite food supplies from Harrison, who now believed that the Prophet was a good influence because he steered the Indians away from alcohol. Cold, hungry, sick, and discouraged by the Prophet's inability to improve their circumstances, some converts gave up and went home. Others would soon arrive to take their places.

They were drawn to Prophetstown as much by Tecumseh's recruiting as by Tenskwatawa's preaching. Tecumseh went to tribes near and far, using every scrap of his skills as an orator and every bit of prestige and honor he possessed, to win support for the intertribal confederation. He did not simply want young firebrands to follow him to Greenville; he wanted wise old chiefs, elderly shamans, and war leaders and policy-makers of all sorts to understand and accept his ideas, to spread those ideas among their own people, and to incorporate the idea of the confederacy into the activities of their communities and tribes. Tecumseh was trying to change the way an entire race thought and acted.

He first preached his cause among the Wyandot and Seneca of northern Ohio. Then he rode west to the Rock and Mississippi rivers, where he met with the Sac, Winnebago, and Fox. He found many believers among these pro-British, anti-American tribes. Some accounts say that he went as far west as Kansas, trying to bring the Osage and other western tribes into the confederacy, but the evidence for this is scanty.

While Tecumseh was recruiting in the west, Harrison took advantage of his absence to buy up some more Indian land. In September 1809, in Fort Wayne, he acquired three million acres from Delaware, Wyandot, and Potawatomi chiefs who were friendly to the government. Harrison assured the chiefs that the U.S. president wanted "no more of your land," but wary Indian leaders such as Tecumseh, as well as many in the U.S. government, knew that the Treaty of Fort Wayne would not be the last treaty. Sooner or later—probably sooner—the whites would want still more land.

The Treaty of Fort Wayne infuriated Tecumseh. He had been working hard to make the Indians see that such sales could not be allowed, and now the traitorous government chiefs had given away still more precious land. Tecumseh, the Prophet, and their followers made many wrathful speeches, declaring that they would take back the land by force and kill the government chiefs if they must. Some of these speeches reached Harrison's ears through his spies. Hoping to quiet the furor at Prophetstown before it erupted into war, he invited the Prophet to Vincennes.

Instead of the Prophet, Harrison was visited by the war chief. Tecumseh accepted the invitation and appeared at Grouseland in the summer of 1810. The meeting began with an angry confrontation and ended in a standoff. Tecumseh insisted that the Treaty of Fort Wayne was not valid; Harrison replied that it would stand.

After the meeting at Grouseland, Harrison wrote to Secretary of War William Eustis, giving an account of the talks he had had with Tecumseh. His description of Tecumseh shows that he was much impressed by the Shawnee chieftain's intelligence and forceful leadership:

> The implicit obedience and respect which the followers
> of Tecumseh give to him is really astonishing, and more
> than any other circumstance bespeaks him as one of
> those uncommon geniuses which spring up occasionally
> to produce revolutions, and overturn the natural order
> of things. If it were not the vicinity of the United States
> he would, perhaps, be the founder of an empire that
> would rival Mexico or Peru. No difficulties deter him.

Tecumseh had informed Harrison that he was in the process of creating a united Indian confederacy that would bring an end to treaty-making. Harrison passed this news on to Eustis, adding what he had learned from his spies and agents about Tecumseh's travels and speeches:

> You see him today on the Wabash, and in a short time hear
> of him on the shores of Lake Erie or Michigan, or on the
> banks of the Mississippi; and wherever he goes he makes

an impression favorable to his purpose. He is now upon
the last round to put a finishing stroke to his work.

The "last round" of which Harrison wrote was Tecumseh's long
trip into the southland. Tecumseh believed that in order to halt
the American advance, the confederacy had to stretch all the way
from the Great Lakes to the Gulf of Mexico. He hoped to find allies
among the southern tribes.

A speech that Tecumseh made in a Choctaw village in Mississippi was probably typical of his oratorical skills. Sam Dale, a
white soldier, heard that speech and later recorded his impres-
sions of the speaker: "His eyes burned with supernatural lustre,
and his whole frame trembled with emotion. His voice resounded
over the multitude—now sinking in low and musical whispers,
now rising to the highest key, hurling out his words like a succes-
sion of thunderbolts. . . . I have heard many great orators, but I
never saw one with the vocal powers of Tecumseh."

To Tecumseh's dismay he found little support among the
Chickasaw and the Choctaw. Some of the younger men were
drawn to his message, but the older chiefs either distrusted
Tecumseh or refused to ally themselves with northern tribes
who were their traditional enemies. Tecumseh's most outspo-
ken opponent was the Choctaw chief Pushmataha, who had
sold large tracts in Mississippi and Alabama to the Americans.
After Tecumseh had made his eloquent plea for a confederacy,
Pushmataha denounced him to the crowd, saying, "I know your
history well. You have ever been a trouble maker. When you
have found yourself unable to pick a quarrel with the white
man, you have stirred up strife between different tribes of
your own race." Pushmataha followed Tecumseh through
Mississippi as the Shawnee leader visited a series of Choctaw
towns. Each time Tecumseh made a speech, the Choctaw leader
threatened to kill anyone of his tribe who joined Tecumseh's
movement.

Seeing that he could accomplish nothing while dogged by the
truculent Pushmataha, Tecumseh left Choctaw territory to carry
his message to the Creek people of Georgia and Alabama. They

Despite his aides' pleas, William Henry Harrison rides boldly into the Battle of Tippecanoe. Harrison later rode into the White House on the strength of his victory over the Indians. *(Photo by C/Z HARRIS from Library of Congress collection)*

responded somewhat more positively both to Tecumseh's message of confederation and to the Prophet's religious teachings as explained by one of his followers who had accompanied Tecumseh to the South. When Tecumseh rode north, about thirty Creek warriors rode with him. Whether the Creek chieftains would join

TECUMSEH AND PUSHMATAHA

In 1811 Tecumseh spoke to a large group of Chickasaw and Choctaw in Mississippi. He urged them to join the confederacy he was trying to create, saying:

> We meet tonight in solemn council—not to debate whether we have been wronged or injured, but to decide how to avenge ourselves. Have we not courage enough to defend our country and maintain our ancient independence?
>
> Where today are the Pequot? Where are the Narragansett, the Mohawk, the Pocanet, and other powerful tribes of our people? They have vanished before the avarice and oppression of the white man, as snow before the summer sun. . . . So it will be with you! Soon their broad roads will pass over the graves of your fathers. You, too, will be driven from your native land as leaves are driven before the winter storms.
>
> Sleep no longer, O Choctaws and Chickasaws, in false security and delusive hopes! Before the white men came among us, we knew neither want nor oppression. How is it now? Are we not being stripped day by day of our ancient liberty? How long will it be before they tie us to a post and whip us, and make us work for them in their fields? Shall we wait for that moment, or shall we die fighting?
>
> Shall we give up our homes, our country bequeathed to us by the Great Spirit, the graves of our dead, and everything that is dear and sacred to us without a struggle? I know you will cry with me: Never! Never! War or extermination is now our only choice. Which do you choose? I know your answer.

When Tecumseh had finished speaking, the Choctaw chief Pushmataha stepped forward. He had made treaties with the whites, and he resented Tecumseh's criticisms of him and the other "government chiefs." Pushmataha believed that the Americans were stronger than the Indians and better equipped to fight a long and bitter war. He did not intend to go into battle against the Americans—and he certainly did not want to see his people

the confederacy should fighting break out, however, was uncertain.

If the lack of support he received in the South was a disappointment to Tecumseh, a far greater disappointment awaited him in the North. Tecumseh had warned Tenskwatawa that Harrison might try to move against Prophetstown while he was away. He had ordered the Prophet not to make war with Harrison under go to war under another man's leadership. He counseled caution:

> I appear before you, my warriors and my people, not to contradict the many charges made against the Americans. The question before us now is not what wrongs they have inflicted upon us, but what measures are best for us to adopt. Reflect, I ask you, before you act hastily. . . . What you are contemplating is a war against a people whose territories are far greater than ours, and who are far better provided with all the implements of war, with men, guns, horses, wealth. . . . Let us not be deluded with the foolish hope that this war, if begun, will soon be over. It will be but the beginning of the end that terminates in the total destruction of our people. Listen to the voice of prudence, O my countrymen, before you act rashly. But whatever you may do, know this—I shall join our friends, the Americans, in this war

Legend says that Tecumseh then called out to the warriors to throw their tomahawks into the air if they meant to follow him to war against the whites. Tomahawks filled the air. In response Pushmataha cried out for all those who agreed with *him* to throw *their* tomahawks into the air, and again the air was filled with tomahawks.

A wise old shaman of the Choctaw was asked to give his opinion on this confusing scene. He said:

> The Great Spirit has asked me to warn you against the dark and evil designs of Tecumseh, and not to be deceived by his words; his schemes are unwise, and if entered into will bring sorrow and desolation upon you and your nations. Choctaws and Chickasaws, obey the words of the Great Spirit.

Tecumseh's plans were not "dark and evil designs." Sadly, however, they would bring "sorrow and desolation" upon his followers, just as the Choctaw shaman predicted.

any circumstances. Tenskwatawa could offer to arrange a meeting, or he could lead his people away to hide in the woods, but he must not fight. Tecumseh had no faith in his brother's ability to conduct a battle. As it happened, his lack of faith was justified.

In the fall of 1811 Harrison led an army of 900 men north to Prophetstown. When the army was camped a few miles from Prophetstown on the banks of the Tippecanoe River,

Tenskwatawa sent a message to Harrison stating that he would meet with the governor the following day. That night Tenskwatawa ordered a surprise attack on the army camp. He promised his followers that spirit magic would protect them, that the bullets of the whites would not hurt them.

The surprise failed. Instead of staging a simple and victorious sneak attack, the Prophet's soldiers found themselves in the middle of a fierce hand-to-hand melee. Despite a slight wound, Harrison galloped about rallying his troops. Tenskwatawa sat some distance away on a rock, chanting magical incantations. The incantations did not work; the soldiers' bullets not only hurt, but killed. Seeing that his attack had failed, Tenskwatawa slunk into the woods, soon to be followed by his remaining troops. The Indians had lost 40 men, the whites 150. The victory in the Battle of Tippecanoe was all Harrison's, however. The governor had broken the believers' faith in the Prophet. And before he left northern Indiana, Harrison burned Prophetstown to the ground.

Soon afterward Tecumseh arrived home. On his way north he had heard the grim news of the Battle of Tippecanoe. Later he recalled his anguish and fury when he saw Prophetstown obliterated: "I stood upon the ashes of my own home, and there I summoned the spirits of the warriors who had fallen. And as I snuffed up the smell of their blood from the ground, I swore once more eternal hatred—the hatred of an avenger!"

Some of that hatred was aimed at Tenskwatawa. Warriors loyal to Tecumseh had planned to kill the discredited Prophet, but Tecumseh declared that Tenskwatawa did not deserve to die. Better to let him live with his shame.

For a time Tenskwatawa tried to reclaim his influence and importance. He retained a few followers who still believed him to be a prophet and holy man. He even attended a few of Tecumseh's councils. But never again would Tenskwatawa command wide respect. His short moment of glory as the spokesman for the Master of Life was over.

Tecumseh's plans for a great confederacy now lay in ashes. Many of his followers had scattered to their former home villages. How

The Battle of Tippecanoe, in which the Prophet promised that the enemy's bullets would be "soft as rain" *(Indiana Historical Society, negative C3806)*

could he hope to unite the tribes when he could not even protect his village? Tecumseh did not give up. He believed that somehow he could draw his followers together again, keep Harrison at bay, and resume the hard task of forging an intertribal confederacy. This time, however, he might accept some help from the British.

NOTES

p. 98   "Who is this pretended . . ." Quoted in R. David Edmunds, *Tecumseh and the Quest for Indian Leadership* (Boston: Little, Brown, 1984), p. 86.

p. 99   "appointed this place . . ." Quoted in Robert Cwiklik, *Tecumseh* (New York: Chelsea House, 1993), p. 65.

p. 99   "bold, commanding, and impassioned." Quoted in Edmunds, p. 97.

p. 101   "shared by all men . . ." Edmunds, p. 97.

p. 101   "all the remaining . . ." Edmunds, p. 109.

p. 104   "no more of your land." Quoted in Edmunds, p. 122.

p. 105   "The implicit obedience . . ." Quoted in Joseph B. Icenhower, *Tecumseh and the Indian Confederation* (New York: Franklin Watts, 1975), pp. 39–41.

pp. 105–6 "You see him today . . ." Quoted in Cwiklik, p. 73.

p. 106   "His eyes burned . . ." Quoted in Cwiklik, pp. 76–77.

p. 106   "I know your history . . ." Quoted in Cwiklik, p. 78.

pp. 108–9 "We meet tonight . . ."; "I appear before you . . ."; and "The Great Spirit . . ." Quoted in *Through Indian Eyes: The Untold Story of America's Native Peoples* (Pleasantville, N.Y.: Reader's Digest Association, 1995), pp. 180–81.

p. 110   "I stood upon . . ." Quoted in Cwiklik, pp. 880–81.

THE END OF
THE DREAM

In 1810, a year before the Battle of Tippecanoe, Tecumseh had told a British agent that his confederation would be complete in one more year. He had told Harrison, too, that he was undertaking his southern trip as the final stage, or "last round," in his great work of creating an intertribal confederacy. Was Tecumseh exaggerating or was he really that close to cementing a confederacy? Had he brought his dream almost to fruition, only to see it collapse after the disaster at Tippecanoe?

Historian Harvey Lewis Carter argues that "Tecumseh's self-imposed task of unification was doomed from the outset, for neither common landownership nor political confederation had any basis in fact among the Indians." Carter continues, "Although Tecumseh worked at confederation, there is no reason to believe that he was as near to accomplishing it as he confidently asserted. The white fear that Tecumseh might succeed was unrealistic, for common sense and a knowledge of Indian tribal government should have told them it could not be done. Indeed, Tecumseh's confederacy was never brought to completion." In Carter's opinion, chieftains such as Little Turtle who encouraged the Indians to assimilate into white society were practical men who looked to the future of their people, while the Shawnee brothers "were backward-looking in their desire to return to Indian ways of an earlier time."

Yet earlier cooperative ventures among Native American tribes had achieved some success. The Iroquois Confederacy, consisting of several tribes under a common government, managed to dominate Indian affairs in the Northeast for many years. Although the member tribes of the Iroquois Confederacy were far closer to one another both culturally and geographically than many of the tribes that Tecumseh hoped to unite, Tecumseh's scheme was not utterly unique. It was simply much more ambitious and far-reaching than any earlier Indian alliance or confederation.

Of course, it is impossible to know how far Tecumseh would have gotten with his plan had the Battle of Tippecanoe and the burning of Prophetstown not occurred. Resistance to change, fear of unleashing the wrath of the American army, and resentment of Tecumseh's leadership would probably have kept many chieftains from joining him—at least at first. Had a war broken out between Tecumseh's followers and the U.S. Army over treaty rights, and had Tecumseh won a few significant victories, then perhaps allies would have streamed to his side from all over North America. Would this have made any real difference to the eventual fate of the Indians and their land? Probably not. The war would have been bigger, longer, and bloodier, but in the end the Americans would have prevailed. They had better numbers and better firepower. Most of all, they had an unquenchable lust for land and an unshakable belief that it was their destiny to rule the continent.

War *did* break out, but it was not the holy war against the Americans that the Prophet and Tecumseh had foretold. It was war between Great Britain and the United States. Once again the Native Americans had to choose sides in a conflict between two alien powers. As the British governor of Canada had written in 1807 when asked about the Indians' role in the event of war, "If we do not employ them, there cannot exist a moment's doubt that they will be employed against us."

In fact, American fears of a British-Indian alliance were one of the causes of the War of 1812. Settlers and officials knew that many of the more militant Indians still maintained friendly links with British agents, traders, and authorities. Some Indian leaders, including Tecumseh, were known to have met with British military and political leaders in the Great Lakes forts and in Canada. As Britain and the United States drew closer to war, Americans in the western territories became increasingly fearful that when war broke out the Indians would ally themselves with the British and attack the frontier settlements.

Such fears were not unfounded. Certainly the Prophet and Tecumseh had been stockpiling British weapons at Prophetstown. Tecumseh had received word from the British in Canada that the British hoped for his support if war broke out. In the spring of 1812 he planned another visit to Canada to discuss with officials the terms of an alliance. Before leaving, however, he had to trick William Henry Harrison into believing that he posed no threat.

After Tippecanoe, Harrison was confident that the Shawnee problem was solved and that the Indians, cowed by defeat, were eager for peace. He wrote to the secretary of war, "I do believe, Sir, that the Indians are sincere in their professions of peace and that we will have no further hostilities." But Harrison became alarmed when warriors began returning to Tecumseh's side. Sensing the imminence of a British-American War, many Kickapoo, Winnebago, and Potawatomi warriors who still respected Tecumseh rejoined him in a new camp built on the ashes of Prophetstown.

To distract Harrison, Tecumseh visited Vincennes again and told the governor that he and his people had no intention of making war. Harrison was further reassured by what happened at a conference between Indian leaders and government officials. A group of Wyandot chieftains there declared that Tecumseh was foolish and that no one would listen to him or follow him. What the officials did not know was that these chieftains secretly supported Tecumseh and were carrying messages to him from the British. Tecumseh had arranged their charade of criticism and abuse to fool Harrison.

The longstanding tension between the United States and Great Britain exploded on June 18, 1812, when Congress declared war. By then Tecumseh was on his way to Canada. He allied himself and his followers with the British and joined their forces at Fort

Malden, a Canadian post at Amherstburg just opposite the American fort at Detroit on the Detroit River.

The American forces based at the fort were commanded by William Hull, a veteran of the American Revolution. No longer young or bold or very sharp, Hull proved a poor commander; for example, he forgot to inform the troops at Fort Mackinac on Lake Michigan that war had been declared. As a result, a British-Indian force easily captured Mackinac in the early days of the war.

Hull tried to invade Canada with 2,200 men but turned back when Tecumseh's Indians fired on his column as it passed through the forest. Despite the Americans' unpromising beginning, however, some Indians speculated that it might be wise to withdraw from their alliance with the British. The Americans, they said, would be back in force. Perhaps the Indians should declare neutrality. Tecumseh countered that the Indians could not afford to remain neutral. They were fighting for their homeland. The British had indicated that, if they won the war, they would look with favor upon an independent Indian nation in the Northwest Territory. Tecumseh declared, "I have taken sides with the king, my father, and I will suffer my bones to lay and bleach upon this shore before I will recross that stream to join in any council of neutrality."

Tecumseh's next action in the war was a prolonged skirmish over a supply train. Around this time a young, confident officer, Major General Isaac Brock, took command of the British forces. In temperament he resembled Tecumseh, and the two men formed a genuine friendship based on mutual admiration and respect. Brock said of Tecumseh, "A more sagacious or more gallant warrior does not, I believe, exist." Tecumseh, impressed by Brock's decisive boldness, informed his followers, "This is a man!"

Brock wanted to attack Fort Detroit. His other officers advised against such a move; Detroit was a strong fort and would be extremely difficult to take. Tecumseh felt it could be done and helped Brock plan the attack.

Brock's troops surrounded Detroit and began shelling the fort. In the meantime, Tecumseh paraded his painted warriors back and forth in front of the Americans. Brock sent a message to Hull warning him that "the numerous body of Indians who have attached themselves to my troops will be beyond my control once the contest commences." There were 1,000 American soldiers in the fort, along with many women and children who had taken refuge there. Brock's men numbered 1,100; Tecumseh's, about 600. Although military historians believe that Hull could have held Detroit, Hull was terrified of an Indian massacre and surrendered on August 16. Brock and Tecumseh had captured Detroit and won an important British-Indian victory. Encouraged by the fall of Detroit and by other British victories elsewhere, still more Indians decided to join Tecumseh on the winning side. Other chieftains and warriors who had allied themselves with the Americans remained loyal.

So far, the war was going Tecumseh's way. In September, however, he lost a friend and ally when Brock was transferred to eastern Canada; Brock was killed in action a month later. Command of the British troops in western Canada went to Colonel Henry Procter, a stuffy and conservative officer who disliked working with Indians.

Although they were fighting the British in the east and south, the Americans also recognized the seriousness of the war on their northwestern frontier. They reorganized the Northwestern Army and appointed a new commander: Tecumseh's old antagonist, William Henry Harrison.

Harrison began by building Fort Meigs on the Maumee River and garrisoning it with 1,800 men. Harrison planned to use Fort Meigs as a base from which to recapture Detroit and then invade Canada. Procter asked Tecumseh to help him attack this fort before Harrison could complete his preparations, and the Shawnee leader agreed. With a combined British-Indian force of 2,000 they surrounded Fort Meigs in April 1813.

Unlike Hull, Harrison did not panic. His confidence reassured his men, who regarded him as a great Indian fighter after his victory at Tippecanoe. Harrison ordered his men to build a series of earthen walls inside Fort Meigs. These barricades greatly

Oliver Hazard Perry encourages American sailors before the Battle of Lake Erie.
(Photo by C/Z HARRIS from Library of Congress collection)

reduced the impact of the artillery shells fired by the British into
the stockade. After four days of bombardment, the British had
accomplished little, and Harrison proclaimed that his men would
defend the fort to their deaths.

The fiercest fighting of the siege of Fort Meigs occurred when
1,200 Kentucky militiamen arrived to reinforce Harrison. Dis-
obeying Harrison's orders, 800 or so of the Kentuckians charged
into the forest, chasing some Indians. Harrison's worst fears were
realized. Indians surrounded the Kentuckians and made short
work of them. Only 150 of the 800 men made it to the fort.

The Indians had captured a number of prisoners, whom they
marched to their camp. There they began slaughtering the prisoners while British officers stood by, unable or unwilling to interfere.
When Tecumseh arrived on the scene and saw what was happening, he flew into a rage, ordered his followers to drop their knives,
and called them cowards for treating helpless prisoners in that

fashion. He also exploded with anger at the British officers who had allowed the carnage to continue.

Procter decided that the siege of Fort Meigs was a failure and ordered a retreat. Another attack on Fort Meigs a few months later also failed. Even worse was a British-Indian attack on Fort Stephenson on the Sandusky River, where fewer than 200 Americans held off a much larger force. Not only had Procter won no significant victories, he had suffered a humiliating defeat. Indians began deserting the British side.

The war was going badly for the British on other fronts as well. Harrison had built a small naval fleet, and in August he launched it on Lake Erie to cut off the supply route to Fort Malden. In a short but immensely significant battle on September 9, 1813, Captain Oliver H. Perry and his nine American ships thrashed the British fleet on the lake, sinking or capturing every British ship.

Harrison and Perry were now ready to join forces, cross the lake, and assault Fort Malden. Rather than stand and fight, Procter determined that it would be prudent to withdraw northward. He invited the Indians to march with him. They responded with hostility and surprise. Why not remain on Lake Erie? Were they not supposed to be fighting for their homeland, not defending Canada? Tecumseh summed up their views in a long speech to

The Battle of Lake Erie was a stunning American victory that frightened Tecumseh's British allies into retreat. *(Photo by C/Z HARRIS from Library of Congress collection)*

"WE WISH TO LEAVE OUR BONES"

When Procter proposed to Tecumseh the retreat from Amherstburg of combined forces, he arranged to have one of his secretaries write down Tecumseh's response so that Procter would have proof of Tecumseh's "insolence." Thus it is that we have a record of what may have been Tecumseh's finest speech.

Tecumseh delivered his last oration in the high-ceilinged council room at Amherstburg. John Richardson, a young British soldier, wrote a description of the Shawnee leader's appearance:

> Habited in a close leather dress, his athletic proportions were admirably delineated, while a large plume of white ostrich feathers, by which he was generally distinguished, overshadowing his brow, and contrasting with the darkness of his complexion and the brilliancy of his black and piercing eye, gave a singularly wild and terrific expression to his features. It was evident that he could be terrible.

Tecumseh began his response to the proposal by reminding Procter that the British had promised to help the Indians defend their homes. He said that the Indians were dismayed to see Procter preparing to run from battle like "a fat animal that carries its tail upon its back; but when affrighted, it drops it between its legs and runs off." Tecumseh closed with a passionate plea:

> Father! You have got the arms and ammunition which our Great Father [the king of England] sent for his red children. If you have an idea of going away, give them to us, and you may go and welcome for us. Our lives are in the hands of the Great Spirit. We are determined to defend our lands, and if it is his will, we wish to leave our bones upon them.

Procter that, says historian R. David Edmunds, was "one of the most inspiring speeches ever delivered by an American Indian." It was a plea to Procter for guns. The Indians, said Tecumseh, meant to stand and fight.

Despite his stirring speech, Tecumseh soon decided to go north with Procter, who claimed that they could make a stand against the Americans at a place called Chatham on the Thames River.

Perry's ships could not sail that far up the river, so Harrison would be on his own. A combined British and Indian force could defeat him. About half of the Indian force—perhaps a thousand men, many of them accompanied by their wives and children—accepted Procter's proposal. The rest scattered back to their homes.

The retreat began in late September, with Harrison's army in pursuit. Procter changed his plans and decided to head for Moraviantown, also on the Thames River, claiming that it would be a better site for the battle. By now the British had pulled far ahead of the slower Indian force. More Indians deserted.

On October 4, Tecumseh and a party of his warriors skirmished with Harrison's troops. Tecumseh received a slight wound on his left arm. Some of Tecumseh's companions later reported that that night, as they made camp, Tecumseh seemed in a somber and thoughtful mood. He reminded them of the journeys they had made together; some of those present had been at his side for a decade. He told them that tomorrow they would face the enemy. He then said that "[h]is father and two of his brothers had died fighting the Long Knives. If the Master of Life willed it, he would join them." In the years to come, this type of eve-of-battle reflection characteristic of any soldier would be twisted into the myth that Tecumseh predicted his own death.

The next morning Tecumseh's 600 or 700 warriors joined Procter's 450 soldiers. Tecumseh sent the Indian women and children away for safety and encouraged his men to fight with honor. By mid-afternoon Harrison's 3,300 troops were upon them. In less than five minutes, Procter and the British troops turned and fled the field without firing a shot from their cannon. Tecumseh and the Indians stood alone against waves of armed horsemen and foot soldiers. When Tecumseh fell, mortally wounded, the surviving Indians fled into the surrounding thickets and forests. The Battle of the Thames was over. So was the dream of an intertribal confederacy and an independent Indian nation.

A few Indian leaders in Canada and Michigan tried to rally the tribesmen to keep fighting the Americans, but the heart had gone out of their struggle. They were discouraged by Tecumseh's

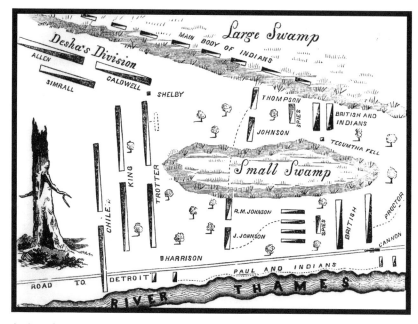

A plan of the Battle of the Thames, Tecumseh's last fight. The words *Tecumtha fell* mark the area where the Shawnee leader died. *(Ohio Historical Society)*

death, by the American victories on Lake Erie and at the Thames, and by Procter's betrayal. Most of them believed that the Americans would win the war, which indeed they did in 1814. The best the Indians of the Old Northwest could now expect was that the Americans would not punish them too severely for their defiance.

The Indian wars were by no means over, not even in the Old Northwest. Fighters such as Black Hawk would continue to take up arms against unfair treaties and broken promises. The Black Hawk War of 1832 was caused in part by a treaty—drawn up by William Henry Harrison in 1804—under which a handful of chiefs gave the government 15 million acres in Illinois, Missouri, and Wisconsin in exchange for annuities of $1,000. But, although the struggle flared up here and there, never again would the Indians of central North America come close to uniting. Never again would they have a leader as fiery, as accomplished, and as visionary as Tecumseh.

Nineteenth-century portraits of Black Hawk, a Sac chieftain who continued the war against American encroachment on Indian lands. A British officer called him "perhaps the ablest and bravest [Indian] since Tecumseh." *(Photo by C/Z HARRIS from* The Black Hawk War, *Chicago, 1903)*

The Shawnee shared the eventual fate of all the tribes. They were forced off their land and either assimilated or driven onto reservations. The tribe had split several times during Tecumseh's lifetime. After his death the remaining Shawnee of the Old Northwest split up again into several bands that migrated off in various directions: to Missouri, to Texas, even to Mexico. Today most Americans of Shawnee descent live in Oklahoma.

Tecumseh's family also wandered in the years after his death. Tenskwatawa had sought refuge in Canada during the War of 1812. He stayed there for ten years, pestering the government and trying to get himself appointed as the guardian of Tecumseh's only surviving son, Pachetha, who had come to Canada with Tecumpease, Tecumseh's and Tenskwatawa's sister. The U.S. government allowed the family to settle in Michigan in 1824, primarily because the governor of the territory, Lewis Cass, was interested in Indian history and wanted to study them. Tecumpease died in Michigan. Tenskwatawa and Pachetha then moved from place to place, finally settling near present-day Kansas City. Before his death in 1837, Tenskwatawa became "something of a tourist attraction as whites stopped by to look at, interview, and sketch the infamous Shawnee prophet about whom there were so many terrible old stories." After Tenskwatawa's death Pachetha went to Texas, where he died in 1840.

Who actually killed Tecumseh? Many in Harrison's army were eager to claim that honor. Several witnesses claimed that Richard Johnson, a militia colonel from Kentucky, fired the shot. Although no one could prove for certain that Johnson had killed the Shawnee leader, the Kentuckian proudly accepted his new nickname, "Old Tecumseh." In later years, after serving in the House of Representatives and the Senate, Johnson ran for vice president under the inspiring campaign slogan:

> Rumpsey dumpsey, rumpsey dumpsey,
> Colonel Johnson slew Tecumseh!

Tecumseh's body was never found—at least, none of the bodies that the Americans found on the battlefield by the Thames River could be positively identified as Tecumseh's. Many years later, some Indians declared that they had carried their fallen leader's body from the field and buried it in a secret grave. Others claimed that the body had been left on the battlefield and was probably one of the many corpses buried by British traders after the American army withdrew. The true fate of Tecumseh's corpse will never be known.

In the years after the death of Tecumseh, people of both races talked and wrote about the fallen war chief. Dozens of those who had known him—or who said that they had known him—rushed to share their stories. Many of the anecdotes about Tecumseh were told by people who had had some contact with him and who later, after he had become famous, realized they could draw a little attention to themselves by telling others of their connection with the renowned chieftain. If these folks touched up their stories a bit when reminiscing, they did no more than many other frontier chroniclers and oral historians were doing at the time.

Some of these stories about Tecumseh, though, were out-and-out lies. If every backwoods frontiersman, soldier, or trader who claimed to have seen, heard, or talked with Tecumseh had really done so, Tecumseh would often have had to be in two or even three places at once. And although there were stories in which Indians claimed that Tecumseh could see in the dark and foretell the future, no one claimed that Tecumseh possessed multiple bodies.

White Americans had feared Tecumseh and bitterly opposed his plans, but after his passing they came to regard him as a hero. Victors often tend to glorify those whom they have defeated, perhaps to make their own victories seem more noble: The greater the foe, the greater the honor in conquering him. During the 19th century, Americans named dozens of towns "Shawnee" or "Tecumseh." Many Indians named their children after Tecumseh, as did some whites, such as the parents of William Tecumseh Sherman, who gained renown as a general in the American Civil War. America's respectful, romantic glorification of Tecumseh was summed up well in an editorial that appeared in an Ohio newspaper a few years after Tecumseh's death:

> Every schoolboy in the Union now knows that Tecumseh was a great man. He was truly great—and his greatness was his own, unassisted by science or the aids of education. As a statesman, a warrior, and a patriot, take him all in all, we shall not look upon his like again.

Today every schoolboy and every schoolgirl does not necessarily know who Tecumseh was. He is less well-known to the general public than Sitting Bull, Geronimo, and other western Indian chieftains are, perhaps because he has been portrayed in fewer movies and television programs. Yet Tecumseh is a hero to Native Americans of all nations—and to everyone who admires integrity and courage.

During Tecumseh's lifetime many whites who knew him or met him sensed that he possessed extraordinary qualities. They called him a man of remarkable brilliance, dignity, and honor. After his death, Native Americans and whites alike embellished these very real qualities and the genuinely striking events of his life with glamorous details, until Tecumseh became a folk hero, as much legend and myth as history.

The real Tecumseh will forever be shrouded in mystery. His people kept no written records. He left no interviews or letters or journals for us to read. There is not even a faded photograph for us to puzzle over. All known accounts of him reach us second- or thirdhand, seen dimly through the turmoil of history and the cloudy confusion of legend. Yet even in this half-darkness Tecumseh shines.

NOTES

p. 113   "Tecumseh's self-imposed task . . ." Harvey Lewis Carter, *The Life and Times of Little Turtle* (Urbana and Chicago: University of Illinois Press, 1987), p. 191.

p. 113   "Although Tecumseh worked . . ." Carter, p. 191.

p. 113   "were backward-looking . . ." Carter, p. 191.

p. 114   "If we do not . . ." Quoted in Robert Cwiklik, *Tecumseh* (New York: Chelsea House, 1993), p. 84.

p. 115   "I do believe, Sir . . ." Quoted in R. David Edmunds, *Tecumseh and the Quest for Indian Leadership* (Boston: Little, Brown, 1984), p. 163.

p. 116   "I have taken sides . . ." Quoted in Cwiklik, p. 86.

p. 116   "A more sagacious . . ." Quoted in Cwiklik, p. 88.

p. 116   "This is a man!" Quoted in Edmunds, p. 177.

p. 117   "the numerous body . . ." Quoted in Edmunds, p. 179.

p. 120   "Habited in a close . . ."; "a fat animal . . ."; and "Father! You have got . . ." Quoted in John Sugden, *Tecumseh's Last Stand* (Norman and London: University of Oklahoma Press, 1985), pp. 54–55.

p. 120   "one of the most inspiring . . ." Edmunds, p. 203.

p. 121   "[h]is father and two . . ." Edmunds, p. 210.

p. 124   "something of a tourist attraction . . ." Bil Gilbert, *God Gave Us This Country* (New York: Atheneum, 1989), p. 331.

p. 126   "Every schoolboy in the Union . . ." Quoted in Gilbert, p. 333.

CHRONOLOGY

▲

	rejects the treaty and begins his quest to unite the tribes against white expansion
1805	Tecumseh's brother Lalawethika transforms himself into Tenskwatawa, the Prophet, launching a Native American spiritual crusade
1808	Tecumseh and Tenskwatawa found Prophetstown, a village on the Tippecanoe River
1809	Treaty of Fort Wayne cedes more Indian land to the whites
1810	Tecumseh meets with territorial governor William Henry Harrison to oppose the Treaty of Fort Wayne
1811	In Battle of Tippecanoe, Harrison defeats Indians led by Tenskwatawa
1812	War breaks out between United States and Great Britain; Tecumseh allies his forces with the British
1813	Tecumseh is killed by Harrison's troops in the Battle of the Thames

SELECTED
FURTHER
READING LIST

▲

Cwiklik, Robert. *Tecumseh: Shawnee Rebel*. New York: Chelsea House, 1993. The story of Tecumseh's life, written for middle-school and high-school students.

Dolan, Terrance. *The Shawnee Indians*. New York: Chelsea House, 1996. An easy-to-read overview of Shawnee culture and history for young readers. Contains two chapters on Tecumseh.

Eckert, Allan W. *A Sorrow In Our Heart: The Life of Tecumseh*. New York: Bantam, 1992. A lively, colorful account of Tecumseh's life and works written by an award-winning author and diligent researcher. In his attempt to create a biography that reads like an exciting novel, Eckert fictionalized or "re-created" scenes and dialogue in many places. Although the author explains his sources and methods for these scenes, readers may be confused about what is established fact and what was made up by the author. Nevertheless, the book is an absorbing read and contains many detailed and fascinating footnotes about people, places, and events of the Old Northwest.

Edmunds, R. David. *The Shawnee Prophet*. Lincoln, Neb.: University of Nebraska Press, 1983. A scholarly biography of Tecumseh's brother that explores the role his spiritual revival played in Indian politics. The author regards Tenskwatawa as a genuine religious leader—not as merely Tecumseh's mouthpiece, as some historians have suggested.

———. *Tecumseh and the Quest for Indian Leadership*. Boston: Little, Brown, 1984. A well-written, scholarly biography of Tecumseh, with emphasis on his attempt to unite Indian peoples into a federation that could hold the line against white encroachment. Young adults may find this book, at 234 pages, perhaps the most readable of all reliable, full-scale biographies of Tecumseh. Of special value is the author's discussion of some often-repeated, yet most likely fictitious, stories about Tecumseh. Edmunds also provides a useful summary of the strengths and weaknesses of many of the books that have been written about Tecumseh, the Prophet, and the Shawnee.

Gilbert, Bil. *God Gave Us This Country: Tekamthi and the First American Civil War*. New York: Atheneum, 1989. A well-written, detailed 369-page text that covers the entire history of Indian resistance in the Great Lakes and Ohio River valley region from the mid-1700s to Tecumseh's death. (The author uses a variant spelling of Tecumseh's name).

Icenhower, Joseph B. *Tecumseh and the Indian Confederation, 1811–1813: The Indian Nations East of the Mississippi Are Defeated*. New York: Franklin Watts, 1975. A book for young adults that looks at Tecumseh's life and deeds in the context of the steady westward expansion of white American settlers and the pressure that this expansion placed on the Indian nations.

Klinck, Carl, ed. *Tecumseh: Fact and Fiction in Early Records*. Englewood Cliffs, N.J.: Prentice-Hall, 1961. A collection of early writings about Tecumseh. Klinck includes a section demonstrating how myths and fictions about Tecumseh have made their way into popular history.

O'Neill, Laurie A. *The Shawnees*. Brookfield, Conn.: Millbrook Press, 1995. A 64-page overview of Shawnee culture and history for young readers that contains a chapter on Tecumseh and the Prophet.

Shorto, Russell. *Tecumseh and the Dream of an American Indian Nation*. Englewood Cliffs, N.J.: Silver Burdett, 1989. Part of Alvin Josephy's biography series of American Indians. Although this easy-to-read 123-page book is true to the major events of Tecumseh's life, it is written in a novel-like form and filled with imagined scenes, conversations, and even thoughts. Such a high degree of fictionalization blurs the line between documentation and imagination.

Stefoff, Rebecca. *William Henry Harrison*. Ada, Okla.: Garrett Educational Corp., 1990. Written for young adults, this biography of Tecumseh's great opponent includes material on Tecumseh, the Prophet, and the Shawnee Confederacy.

Sugden, John. *Tecumseh's Last Stand*. Norman, Okla.: University of Oklahoma Press, 1985. A detailed, 286-page account of the Battle of 1812 from the point of view of the Indians and their British allies. A good resource for any reader interested in learning more about the hard-fought war that many historians dismiss as a "small naval conflict."

Sword, Wiley. *President Washington's Indian War: The Struggle for the Old Northwest, 1790–1795*. Norman, Okla.: University of Oklahoma Press, 1985. Readers interested in military history will find this book full of fascinating details about the first American federal army and the campaigns of Generals Harmar and St. Clair.

Walker, Paul Robert. *Spiritual Leaders*. New York: Facts On File, 1994. A collective biography written for young adults; includes one chapter on Tenskwatawa.

INDEX

▲

Page numbers in *italics* indicate illustrations.

W

Wabash River 1, 2–3, 21, 57, 103, 105

Wapakoneta (Shawnee settlement) 87, 99

War Department 5, 8, 69, 72

War of 1812 12, 114, 124

Washington, D.C. 4, 10

Washington, George 13, 39, 48, 50, 68, 69
    and St. Clair 55, 59–60, 61, 63, 65

Wayne, Anthony 69–77, 70, 73, 79

West Virginia 15, 27, 29

White River 83, 84, 89

Williamson, David 50, 51

Winamac (Potawatomi chieftain) 3, 8

Winnebago Indians 9, 104, 115

Wisconsin 12, 103, 122

Wyandot Indians 9, 18, 50, 103, 115
    allied with Shawnee 41, 54, 75, 97, 104